Beyond Academic Departments

The Story of
Institutes and Centers

Stanley O. Ikenberry

Renee C. Friedman

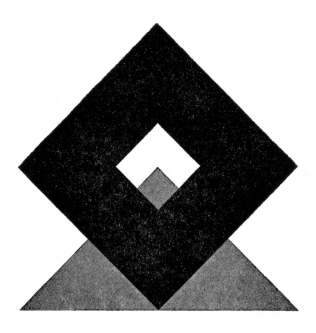

BEYOND
ACADEMIC
DEPARTMENTS

Jossey-Bass Inc., Publishers
San Francisco · Washington · London · 1972

The Jossey-Bass
Series in Higher Education

Consulting Editor

HAROLD L. HODGKINSON
University of California, Berkeley

Preface

Colleges and universities are curious institutions, not well understood by those who spend their lives in them and even less understood by society at large. Most who have attended a college or university, however, and nearly all who have worked as members of a faculty or in an administrative capacity know that the life of the academy revolves around the department. Although the institution, over time, can determine which departments it sponsors, the departments once created tend to shape the goals and character of the institution. Some may criticize departments, but few dispute their powerful position within the academic organization.

Following World War II, however, some institutions, particularly the large, complex universities, began to move beyond departments. It was a period of growth: enrollments, buildings, faculty size and breadth of competence, budgets, fund sources, constituencies, programs, goals, and purposes—everything seemed to get bigger and more complex. And the organizational structures of colleges and universities were no exception. New offices, bureaus, centers, laboratories, and institutes emerged on the organizational chart alongside the conventional departments.

In many ways these new organizations were like departments. They employed professional personnel with similar if not identical qualifications. Many were very clearly engaged in the work of the academy—teaching, research, or service. In other obvious ways, however, they were quite different. They didn't focus on a single discipline, as did departments. Funding tended to come principally from grants and contracts with foundations, governments, businesses, or industries, and not from the traditional sources. And there seemed to be a tentativeness to the whole enterprise—less permanence of programs, staff, budget, and other resources than one tended to expect in departments.

The new structures proved to be attractive to faculty members, administrators, and donors. Once a minor and generally insignificant appendage, institutes grew in number and scope of operations in universities and colleges until they controlled a significant segment of the programs and resources at many institutions and rivaled departments in numbers. As they multiplied, they tended frequently to become centers of controversy. Split appointments, different budget constraints, different policies, and different values widened the gulf between departments and institutes on many campuses.

The initial impetus to study institutes and centers as an organizational phenomenon came from G. Lester Anderson, director of the Center for the Study of Higher Education at Pennsylvania State University. It was reinforced by discussions with Paul L. Dressel of Michigan State University, who had just completed a careful study of the functioning of academic departments and had included in his study a small number of centers and institutes for comparative purposes.

We had several reasons for looking at institutes and their origins, structure, and functioning. Institutes and centers constitute a much larger share of operations on many campuses than anyone imagines. They have grown rapidly and largely without a grand design. Their programs are frequently criticized but almost never studied and understood. And their directors have little to guide their actions other than their own intuition and academic good sense. We felt that an examination of institutes and centers, such as the one presented here, could be useful to those associated with them and to those who must relate to them—administrators, faculty members, department chairmen, deans, and governing boards, as well as foundations, governments, and other external sponsors.

In addition, there are growing pressures for universities and colleges to improve their functioning, to consolidate their typically fragmented organizational structure, and to find new organizational solutions to old and familiar problems. Because resources are limited, many institutions find themselves in a period of reassessment and retrenchment. Institutes and centers cannot avoid becoming the focus of attention during this period. Our hope is that *Beyond Academic Departments* will enable institutes and centers and the universities and colleges of which they are a part to cope with the demands of the times wisely and effectively.

One pauses at the conclusion of writing a book to thank the many individuals who made it possible. Our colleagues at the Center for the Study of Higher Education were helpful in ways possible only when friends share a day-by-day intellectual kinship, giving and challenging ideas. Kenneth Mortimer, Larry Leslie, Lester Anderson, and others played such a role. John Frey, director of the Institute for Research on Land and Water Resources, and his research assistant, Marvin Swope, played especially important roles, for they initiated a large-scale study of the operation of the national network of fifty-one water centers throughout the country at about the same time our study was getting under way. The possibility of collaboration with Dr. Frey and our mutual interest in land grant universities led us to work quite closely together over the months that followed. Mary Norman, then a graduate student at Pennsylvania State, also contributed to our effort by conducting much of the literature search and a survey-case study of the nearly forty institutes and centers on the Pennsylvania State campus. Our thanks go to Richard Cunningham, Harry Zook, and Robert Friedman— all of Pennsylvania State—who reviewed the manuscript at various stages and gave us useful criticism. Our appreciation also goes to Jane Peterson for her editorial suggestions, to Sandra Rothrock and Susan Rogacs, whose secretarial skills were invaluable in the preparation of the manuscript, and to others who gave freely of their time and assistance.

Perhaps our greatest thanks, however, should go to those

more than 125 institute and center directors who so carefully responded to our inquiries and to the more than forty university administrators who took time from their busy schedules to respond in writing and by telephone to our questioning. Without their help, any systematic effort to examine institutes and centers would have been impossible.

September 1972   STANLEY O. IKENBERRY
University Park, Pennsylvania   RENEE C. FRIEDMAN

Contents

Contents

Beyond Academic Departments

The Story of Institutes and Centers

Beyond Departments

Among the most interesting changes in American colleges and universities over the past quarter of a century is the rather prolific growth of institutes, centers, laboratories, bureaus, and other research and service units that parallel the conventional departmental structure. No easy description of these additions to the academic landscape is possible. They carry out a bewildering variety of purposes, use many different organizational models, are supported at widely disparate levels of investment, are sometimes housed in the obscure corners of the campus, and are found at all levels of the organizational hierarchy. The purpose of this book is to explore this diversity in origin, function, and structure and the relationships of institutes and centers to the university.

Today's complex higher education institution bears scant resemblance to its seventeenth-, eighteenth-, or nineteenth-century counterparts. These earlier institutions, by contemporary standards, were small. Their programs of study were relatively elementary. And their functions were reasonably well defined, centered on the instruction of undergraduates. Their students came from comparatively homogeneous economic and social backgrounds and were taught by a faculty with little academic training beyond the baccalaureate level. But much has changed for the contemporary multiversity.

In the intervening centuries, universities have adapted themselves to the changing economic, social, and technological structure of society. The complex institution no longer concentrates principally on teaching undergraduate students, although this responsibility is still important. Universities have taken on new functions and have formed new priorities and emphases which respond to societal pressures and to the value systems and judgments of academic professionals within the institutions themselves. Although conceptions of mission and the blend of functions vary from institution to institution, increasing emphasis has been placed on research; graduate education; solving the scientific, technological, and social problems of society; and establishing direct service relationships between the university and the community.

American society now knows the utility of universities and has transformed them into immense centers of power. Universities have found it difficult to turn their heads and pass by an opportunity to take on expanded functions. Yet they also have found it difficult to accommodate new functions within the traditional academic structure, and institutes and centers have emerged as alternative means to this accommodation. Perhaps more than five thousand such units are now operating on American campuses; most have begun their work since World War II.

The growth of institutes has not been without controversy. Some view their growth as overly opportunistic, as evidence of an excessive enthusiasm on the part of universities to be all things to all people. There have been clashes between the apparent purposes served by some institutes and the goals and objectives of the universities of which they are a part. This conflict, in turn, has contributed to the view that institutes and the organized research and service they carry out are somehow at the root of the general confusion over goals and objectives that plagues higher education.

The impact of institutes and centers on the changing character of American colleges and universities is a genuine concern.

2

Beyond Departments

Some people question whether the societal needs filled by institutes and centers are met most appropriately within the context of a university. And if so, how should the university be organized to carry out these expanded, multiple functions effectively? Still another question relates to the conflict and competition among priorities. Like other units within the university, institutes drain institutional resources. Faculty members, department chairmen, and deans have occasionally claimed that institutes weaken the institution as a whole by draining resources and programs away from the core of the university—its academic departments. The issue has become more salient as financial strains have increased.

If program cutbacks are to be effected, what are the priorities? Should institutes and centers take the first round of cuts? As federal funds are reduced, should increased institutional funds be allocated to institutes to take their place? What financial and operational security should an institute expect? In times of financial crisis, should institutes and departments be treated alike? Answers to these questions are far from clear in many colleges and universities.

University policies on institutes are not well developed. This deficiency stems partly from the rapid diffusion of goals in universities and the comparatively recent appearance of institutes in significant numbers. Policies related to the employment and promotion of professional personnel are perhaps the best developed. Most institutions maintain dual personnel policies, one applicable to professional employees in academic departments and the other applicable to professional employees in institutes. Such personnel policies suggest a basic assumption: that institute objectives and programs are somehow not in harmony with or are at least different from the values of departments and colleges.

Additional questions are raised by the comparative geographic and organizational isolation of institutes. They are many times cut off from the main lines of formal and informal communication. Bringing institutes into the university, making them *of* the university and not merely *at it,* is a genuine organizational dilemma. The problem stems from additudinal as well as organizational and

3

policy issues. It is related to the haphazard manner in which institutes and centers have emerged on most campuses. The nontraditional and occasionally debatable functions that institutes serve also encourage isolation and a we-they approach to university life.

Many universities, public as well as private, face periods of severe stress. All universities, even those not under stress, must reexamine their programs and redefine the place of institutes and centers within the organizational structure. During what may be an extended period of financial belt-tightening, many university programs—departments as well as institutes—will be cut back, merged, reoriented, or phased out in order to avoid placing an intolerable drain on essential resources. How can obsolete institute programs be phased out and changes in emphasis be brought about? How can room be made for new institutes needed to solve tomorrow's problems? How can the needed institutional flexibility and relevance be achieved? The challenges with which colleges and universities are bombarded demand new programs to serve new ends.

Institutes tend to be organized around tasks that, in contrast to those of academic departments, may involve more than one discipline. This essential difference, although elementary, is at the root of the added flexibility provided by their organizational form. Few indications suggest that institutes will replace academic departments in the foreseeable future as the principal university organizational mode. Neither, however, is there evidence that demands for a task-oriented or mission-oriented posture on the part of universities will lessen. Thus, institutes are likely to continue to add a useful dimension to the overall organizational configuration. The issue is how institutes and centers can become more effective, better serve the purposes of the university as well as their own, and become more fully integrated in the life of the institution than they now are.

A logical first step is to examine their origins. Much initiative has come from outside the university, particularly from the federal government, which has invested enormous sums of money in universities since World War II, much of it in institutes and centers. Many of them, such as the national network of institutes for water resources research, have come about largely in response to federal legislation. Other units have been born in the hope that they will attract federal support. Special interest groups in agriculture, business, industry, and education have sought new services from the university and, in many instances, have been willing to pay for them.

From these external forces emerged a new breed of academic entrepreneur. If knowledge has been for sale, he has been the vendor. In some cases the institute or center may provide an open environment for the faculty entrepreneur to "do his thing." Perquisites such as travel, time for research, secretarial assistance, space, and graduate assistants may come his way more quickly in the institute, in which he can pay his way, than in the department, where reasonable parity must be maintained. Thus, initiative from a strong faculty member or group of faculty who see establishing a center as a means to advance their personal careers is a factor to be considered. Another source has been university administrators who were instrumental in establishing institutes. What were their motives, and to what extent were their purposes served? And what blend of interactions between and among forces—internal and external—led to the proliferation of institutes?

A second focus of this study is the nature and variety of institute functions. Many carry out instruction, research, or public service functions. One distinctive quality which differentiates the institute from the academic department is that its activities tend to be more precisely defined and restricted. The department, as the basic element in the university organizational structure, has grown increasingly important as academic professionalism has gained ascendance. Although it performs many tasks, the department is not task-oriented; it is organized around a discipline that can be applied to any number of tasks. Departments typically engage in a wide variety of functions at all levels of instruction, in the area of research, and in public service. Do institutes with their more restricted mandate present a more attractive option as universities move toward program, planning, and budgeting systems? In short, what is the range of functions carried out by institutes and centers?

5

Beyond Academic Departments

What is the pattern? And what comparisons can be made with academic departments?

One would expect the variation in organizational structure to equal the variation in function. Some institutes are immense organizations, massive bureaucracies having all the resources necessary for self-sufficiency. Other centers maintain only a skeletal staff, such as a talented director and a few key part-time staff members. A third class of institutes, sometimes referred to as paper institutes, tend to be assembled on an ad hoc, demand basis. They exist, as organizational realities, only when needed. What is the impact of these different structures in relation to employment policies and practices, power and authority relationships, and space, budget, and equipment requirements?

Power in the university usually resides in the academic departments, schools, and colleges, and these units have been reasonably effective in influencing the development of institutes. Instruments of departmental power include control of faculty appointments, academic rank, salaries, promotions, and tenure. Centers can also deal in perquisites, including time, money, and status. An understanding of the balance of power between departments and institutes is essential to an understanding of the current position of institutes within the university.

The present university structure, taken as a whole, tends to be poorly integrated and not always rational in design. Universities too frequently appear to be loose collections of competing departments, schools, institutes, centers, programs, and committees, sometimes uncommunicative and too often uncoordinated. The organizational position of institutes and centers varies widely among universities and within the university structure. Some units enjoy independent status similar to that of a school or college; others are incorporated within the framework of a college or department. Or the institute may be an independent corporation, tied to the university only by physical location, overlapping board membership, or common staff. This variety again raises the obvious question of how institutes and centers can be integrated directly with the mainstream of the university structure.

6

Beyond Departments

To provide a basis for looking at these questions and issues, we gathered data from several sources. A descriptive profile of some 900 institutes and centers located at fifty-one land-grant universities showed the number and diversity of such units in these institutions (Ikenberry, 1970). In addition, a review of forty-four institutes located at a single university presented the origins and interrelationships of institutes on a single campus (Norman, 1971). A series of semistructured telephone interviews with university administrators in twenty-five land-grant universities gave still a third perspective. The bulk of the information, however, was obtained from 125 institute directors who described the origin, structure, function, and general characteristics of the institutes they directed in fifty-one land-grant universities. Their replies were supplemented by responses of university administrators regarding institutional policies related to professional personnel employed in institutes as well as administrative attitudes toward institutes. The results of these various studies are not reported separately but have been merged in the report that follows.

The decision to concentrate on institutes and centers in land-grant universities was made for several reasons. Although these institutions are not representative of all universities, there is considerable diversity among them. Geographically, they span the nation. Academically, they range from the eminent to the relatively obscure. And, as a group, land-grant universities constitute a definable class of institutions, with certain traditions of applied research and public service in common.

The institutes and centers chosen for study included fifty centers of a single type—the national network of water centers— and seventy-five other institutes in the social, physical, and life sciences. Attention was directed at the fifty water centers for several reasons. First, the water center is the single institute common to all land-grant institutions in the sample and thus provides an opportunity to examine interinstitutional variations within this single class of centers. Second, the dynamics of interaction between the federal government and higher education is well illustrated in this national network. These centers grew largely in response to the

7

Water Resources Act of 1964, which called for the establishment of one water center in each state and Puerto Rico.

The seventy-five additional institutes incorporated in the study were by no means chosen randomly but reflected the following considerations: the description of the institute suggested that it was not simply an equipment depository or a departmental "holding company"; it appeared to be an actual organization, with evidence of at least some budgetary support and staff; and the unit was an integral part of the university, not a separately organized unit outside the corporate structure. The *Research Centers Directory* (Palmer, 1968) was the basic source for selecting institutes to be studied. Since much of their growth has occurred relatively recently, most units selected were formed in the last two decades, but some older and better established institutes were also deliberately included. Although all university functions—instruction, research, service— are carried out in some form by some institutes, we emphasized research- and public service-oriented institutes as opposed to special instructional centers or continuing education programs. Agricultural and engineering experiment stations were excluded, although these units were among the first "institutes" established on university campuses.

We contacted the president of each of the fifty-one universities in which a water center was located and asked whether his institution would participate in the study. He was also asked to designate a member of the central administrative staff such as a vice-president for research, academic vice-president, or other central administrative officer to serve as spokesman on questions of institutional policy. Affirmative replies were received from all fifty-one presidents.

Letters were also sent to the director of each water center, to directors of sixty-seven institutes in the social sciences and humanities, and to directors of sixty institutes in the area of the physical and life sciences. The letter requested permission to include the particular institute in the study and asked the director to complete a questionnaire dealing with the origins, structure, functions, and general characteristics of the institute. Completed and usable

8

questionnaires were received from fifty directors of water resources centers, a return of 98 per cent. Response rates were lower in other areas, with forty-three of the sixty-seven directors of social science and humanities institutes responding, a return of 64 per cent. In the case of physical-life science institutes, thirty-two of the sixty directors responded with usable material, a return of 53 per cent. Despite the care taken in selecting research centers and institutes, many turned out to be nonexistent, nonfunctioning, or extinct.

University administrators designated as institutional representatives were sent a two-part questionnaire. The first section dealt with university policies regarding the employment of professional personnel in institutes and centers. The second portion contained fifteen statements which compared the functional advantages of institutes with those of academic departments. Fifty-one administrators were contacted, and usable responses were received from forty-six of them, a return of 90 per cent. Two administrators indicated that their university did not sponsor any institutes as such, and another declined to participate in the study. An additional two questionnaires, for various reasons, were not usable.

After receiving the questionnaire responses, we conducted telephone interviews with the university administrators from twenty-five of the participating institutions. The interviews were designed to be informal and open-ended and to probe deeply into the origins, functions, and structure of institutes and centers. We tried to tap the judgments of administrators regarding the future of institutes on their campuses and to get at responses they might have been hesitant to place in writing.

Added to these data are impressions, gleaned from our experiences and from the experiences of others, that make this book more than a research report and perhaps cause it to raise more questions than it answers. Yet the lack of solutions does not detract from our purpose: to improve the functioning of higher education as an essential partner in our society.

Many institutions are reexamining the role of institutes and centers. The fundamental purposes of universities are being questioned, and institutes are the focus of much of the debate. Universities, in effect, serve as the auxiliary research wings of corporations and governments or, as DeWitt and Tussing (1971, p. 3) put it, as the "Kelly girls" of the research area. Frequently they do so to the genuine benefit of all. They provide an elastic supply of highly trained and well-equipped research and service talent and at the same time give valuable training to graduate students. On occasion, however, their efforts are more responsive to the needs of others than to their own. Reexamination of basic university purposes will eventually determine the proper place of institutes in the overall structure.

II

Origins

Universities are principal suppliers of fuel for social, economic, and technological innovation in our society, and the rate of consumption of that fuel has grown at an unbelievable pace. The growing demands for research and public service, as well as education, have undoubtedly contributed to the proliferation of institutes and centers. Any examination of their origins must focus on the increased dependence of society on science and the products of science, as well as on the concomitant escalation of the research function in universities.

Attention must also be given to the professional and personal motives of faculty members who may view the establishment of an institute or center as useful in satisfying their immediate or long-term career needs and ambitions. At one extreme, institutes have enabled individual scholars to pursue their work effectively; at the other, institutes have fed the ambitions and exploited the talents of a new breed of academic entrepreneur.

Another force in the proliferation of institutes is the concern of university administrators for institutional change and development. While society attempts to serve its purposes and faculty members work to satisfy their career demands by creating institutes and centers, administrative response to problems frequently includes the creation of new organizations designed to deal with them. Many institutes have emerged through this route.

The results of this study suggest that some measure of support from each of the three major sources—society, faculty, and university administrators—was present in the establishment of most institutes. The forces leading to the creation of these units also suggest the expectations for them and the criteria with which they are evaluated.

The University and Society

The importance of research was quite apparent to the academic community in 1954, when an American Council on Education report declared:

> *The financial support of research cannot be considered adequately without feeling the importance of research in our national life. It has come to be a major means for furtherance of our national objectives and for the maintenance of the general welfare and the national safety. It has come to exert a great influence on our economy. . . . Research has come to play a fundamental part in the maintenance of the public health. . . . Similarly, research is essential to national defense. . . . For these clearly evident reasons, it has become national policy to encourage and support research, and the growing conviction of the American people that research is essential to their welfare underlies the action of our government in making federal funds available on a scale that would have hardly been imagined a quarter of a century ago [p. 74].*

Prior to 1940, federal aid for university research was modest and very largely confined to argiculture, but during that decade the government began the first significant support of research in areas related to defense and health, providing a wide group of universities with substantial amounts of money. It raised the level of its support in the cold war period (Rivlin, 1961, p. 24). The *rate* of increase

12

has been especially dramatic. Using a base of 100 to indicate the 1953 level, March reports a rise to 204 by 1959, to 546 by 1965, and to 801 by 1970 (1970, p. 2). Inflation reduced the impact of these massive increases, but it is nonetheless apparent that increased federal support, in combination with the growing reliance on universities by state governments, private foundations, business, and industry, contributed very substantially to a major redefinition of the role of research in the university. The emergence of research institutes reflected, in part, attempts by institutions to accommodate this newly defined mission.

Certain institutes were established directly as a result of legislation. Water resources legislation was an influential factor, for example, in the establishment of most water centers—nearly two-thirds of the directors, 64 per cent, report that this legislation had a significant effect. This finding is supported by the fact that 58 per cent ranked "evidence of significant financial support or the strong probability thereof from grantors or constituent groups" as the foremost influence in the establishment of their centers. Whether societal influence was directly responsible for the creation of institutes, as in the case of the water centers, or whether it was subtle, it nonetheless played a fundamental role. It also set in motion other external forces that contributed in their own ways to the proliferation.

The realization that research was useful and perhaps even essential to the continued progress of an advanced industrial society required adaptation in the organization as well as the mission of universities. The American people, through Congress, gave vigorous support to university research primarily as a means of achieving particular ends (Haworth, 1966, p. 44). This utilitarian or task-oriented posture, however, was not and is not a primary controlling element in the organizational design of universities. The apparent aloofness of the academic department from a specific problem-solving orientation is suggested by the somewhat impish comment that "society has its problems and universities have their departments." However, the implicit assumption underlying social support for research is that society has the right to expect the devotion of universities to the solution of its problems.

Research sponsors, including the federal government, frequently are convinced that their particular tasks or missions can best be accomplished by a unit independent from academic departmental control. This conviction was apparent in the establishment of the network of water centers. The initial guidelines for submission of proposals made clear the preference that these units be established outside the conventional departmental structure. As a result, none of these centers was established in a department, and 90 per cent are independent of schools and colleges as well.

Rivlin (1961) observes that "almost without exception, present federal programs provide funds only for specific purposes." Speaking of categorical aid, Rivlin goes on to suggest that "the effect of this federal earmarking is to distort college and university programs into patterns the institutions would not themselves have chosen" (p. 160). Indeed, many governmental and foundation grantors have aimed openly to influence the purposes and character of an institution in directions they judged appropriate. Grantors throughout the ages have sought to ensure increased dedication of the university to their values and to the achievement of their tasks. In many instances the tasks are those most would judge worthy, such as curing cancer, educating the mentally retarded, solving the problems of state and local government. The creation of task-oriented, special-purpose institutes and centers provides many grantors additional assurance that their resources will be used to pursue their goals rather than the general objectives of the university.

One of the most widely accepted and frequently cited reasons for the creation of institutes is the increased demand for multidisciplinary or interdisciplinary collaboration. The commitment to solve certain social or technological problems introduced the prospect that the talents required for a particular task would range beyond the capacity of a single discipline or department. Research and development work in the space program required not only the talents of engineers, physicists, and mathematicians but those of biologists, geologists, chemists, electronic technologists, metallurgists, economists, psychologists, and sociologists, not to mention accountants, public relations experts, and television specialists. Curing cancer, eradicating poverty, and stopping pollution demand a variety of disciplines. As Jencks and Riesman (1968) observe, clients' problems, real or imaginary, rarely fall into neat departmental categories. One might add that when they do, the beauty is more likely to be in the eye of the beholder, as men tend to define tasks in terms of their conceptual frame of reference and their personal competencies.

Academic departments, by definition, resemble guilds to which admission depends on a reasonable congruence of the candidate's disciplinary training and conceptual and methodological orientation with the majority view of the department. Cross-disciplinary appointments are made, as in the employment of a psychologist by a department in education or a mathematician by an engineering department, but the number of such appointments is not large. Sufficient difficulties are encountered in split appointments that some universities limit or openly discourage them.

Nonetheless, many faculty members work across departments on an informal basis. A mathematician and an economist, for example, may collaborate informally on a project of joint interest. The department of civil engineering may administer an externally funded project for which the part-time services of a sociologist are required. The sociologist, however, is likely to remain employed full-time in the sociology department. Such arrangements are possible, and those who are skeptical or critical of the institute or center as an organizational form frequently cite the success of such relationships in defense of their position.

Informal collaboration among a limited number of departments involving a small number of faculty members for a limited period of time can be easily accommodated within the conventional structure. But the escalation of the research function in the university and increased demand for the application of academic talents to the solution of social and technical problems have led to the emergence of multimillion-dollar research and service programs involving hundreds of individuals from scores of academic depart-

15

ments. An institute, center, or laboratory provides an apparently neutral ground on which faculty with different departmental allegiances can work together and an organizational structure responsive to the magnitude and complexity of the task.

The vice-president for graduate studies of a major land-grant university provided a good illustration of the interaction of these external forces by initiating a center for materials research on his campus. The Department of Defense had provided major financial support for materials research for the physics department. As time moved on, the federal agency became concerned that its goals were not being met. A representative from the federal agency conveyed its concern to the university president and suggested that research support might be withdrawn, or at least sharply reduced in the future. The president referred the matter to the vice-president for graduate studies, who, in turn, persuaded a prestigious member of the chemisty department to draft a proposal for the establishment of an autonomous, multidisciplinary research center. The proposal attempted to demonstrate the interdisciplinary quality of the proposed unit, to assure that the physics department could no longer dominate the allocation of research resources, and to suggest that faculty members in other departments would play ball. The sponsor was persuaded, and the center was funded at a very substantial level.

Rossi (1964) suggests that the teaching function in universities needs only rudimentary supervision in a bureaucratic or organizational sense. Certainly few would maintain that it receives much more. A considerable measure of autonomy can be, and some would argue must be, granted to the individual professor in the conduct of his affairs.

Organized or team research, however, demands increased organizational control. The research function, especially large-scale, task-oriented research involving the effort of several individuals, tends to need a different climate and structure. A clear division of labor among professionals and between professionals and supporting personnel is required. Men must frequently pace their work with others in accord with a predetermined schedule in which the initiation of one phase of the project is dependent on the successful com-

16

pletion of earlier work. The task may be rather clearly defined in a scope of work statement which has been legally consummated in the form of a contract. The net effect of these requirements is to establish boundaries and to define interpersonal relationships within which individuals must operate. This type of research calls for a bureaucratic organizational unit which enables precise division and specialization of labor; clear definition of hierarchical authority relationships; and increased attention to efficiency, coordination, and control. Rossi suggests that the organizational tensions between the teaching and research functions in universities have been resolved, in part, by segregating large-scale, organized research programs in units especially designed for that purpose—institutes and centers (p. 1146).

Career Needs of Faculty

The motives and concerns of faculty members in the establishment of institutes and centers cannot be fully understood without acknowledging the rapid growth of academic professionalism in higher education during the twentieth century and particularly since World War II. The substantial effect of the goals and values of professionalism can be observed in nearly every aspect of modern university life—in faculty recruitment, promotion, and tenure; in the selective admission of students, the curriculum, and teaching loads and course assignments; in the status accorded teaching; in budget decisions and all aspects of resource allocation; and, more basically, in the concept of the mission of colleges and universities and the defined role of faculty members in the achievement of that mission. Professionalization, in essence, was the *Academic Revolution* of which Jencks and Riesman (1968) wrote. The result has been the assignment of high value to the creation of knowledge and of a low priority to the mere transmission of knowledge.

Ascendance of the value of research has also led to the increased importance of research productivity as a criterion for judging the professional competence of faculty. When teaching loads were relatively heavy and research support slight, research

17

productivity could be viewed as evidence of unusual professional vitality. But the rapid escalation in the availability of research support since 1950 and the corresponding reduction in faculty teaching loads have shifted the burden of proof of competence to the faculty member. Failure to gain access to research resources, including time, materials, graduate assistants, secretarial help, travel support, space, and equipment, may not only restrict research productivity but may significantly influence career advancement.

Some faculty members apparently believe that access to research resources is more readily available in a research institute or center than in an academic department. For this reason they may work for the establishment of an institute or they may fight it for fear that research resources available to the department may be reduced. In either case, professional values, including the ascending priority assigned to the research function, the expectation of research productivity, and its use in judging professional competence, are involved.

Another factor is the increased career satisfaction that may be available to selected faculty members through directing or working in an institute. Rand (1964) hints at this when he observes that centers are usually headed by scholar-entrepreneurs who have much in common with college presidents of earlier years. He notes that they can "manage personnel, plan campaigns, and deal with foundations," whereas opportunities for such activities may be somewhat restricted in conventional departments. Rand goes on to suggest that they use their tools to increase their effectiveness as scholars and academic leaders in the outside world (p. 75). He describes the phenomenon as a third class of career, neither solely academic nor solely administrative (p. 93).

The academic department may, at times, frustrate or inhibit a faculty member's initiative, sometimes at a critical point in his career. The directorship of an institute or center may provide an attractive substitute to the departmental chairmanship—already filled by an individual not near retirement—or a pseudo-deanship for the individual whose career needs include a blend of the academic and administrative.

Origins

For those who seek it, the directorship is not without elements of power. Ability to work with funding agencies and success in generating external support can produce increased personal power and prestige. The ability to control access to research support affects the distribution of rewards and sanctions on a campus, tending to ascribe influence to those who have such control.

While not all professional staff members of an institute have access to leadership positions, they may nonetheless receive certain perquisites such as travel support, graduate assistants, funds for and assistance in data collection, and secretarial help not so readily available in a department. Appointments may be on a twelve-month rather than a nine-month basis, and staff may have not only greater time for research but greater assistance in publishing their findings.

Help in preparing grant applications and in getting external support for research can be a very important benefit. A large fraction of effort, whether in a department or in a center, is frequently devoted to drafting grant applications, preparing progress reports, making arrangements for site review teams, bookkeeping, purchasing, and other frenetic activities. Although access to a research center does not relieve these burdens, faculty members may be closer there than in a department to those who know the ropes. In large institutes, special staff may be available to take over certain of these chores, performing a very real service.

Institutional Development

The obvious impact of increased federal funding and categorical aid and the rather strong pressures from some members of the faculty may lead some to believe that institutes have emerged largely as a result of the forces of exploitation from outside the university and of opportunism from within. If so, it must also be noted that university administrators played a key role in the creation of institutes and centers in nearly every case studied.

Because the authorization and creation of a new unit, whether a department or an institute, is almost certain to place an additional drain on university resources, it is important to ask why

19

administrators permit, and sometimes even take the initiative in, the creation of institutes. Interviews with university administrators revealed eight concerns or motives related to their decisions. These concerns, for the most part, centered around strategies for institutional development, such as recruitment and retention of faculty members; increased coordination and communication among departments and programs; strengthened graduate education and research programs; resolution of internal conflicts; establishment of new institutional goals; renovation and reform of existing departments; creation of special areas of academic emphasis and specialization; and enhancement of institutional visibility and prestige. Each of these administrative concerns is discussed here.

Faculty aspirations to initiate, direct, or be part of an institute—for whatever motives—make institutes and centers useful in a general institutional effort to recruit and retain able faculty members. Several instances of this concern were revealed, but two examples illustrate the point. In the mid-1960s, the vice-president for research of a university in the Southwest, aware that a major oil company was cutting back on its research units, reasoned that a research team, headed by an internationally recognized chemist, might be persuaded to join the university. Negotiations among the chemists, the research team, and the chief executive of the oil company led to the establishment of a special research institute to attract and accommodate the team.

Another southwestern university was attempting to strengthen its economics department and had earlier recruited two highly rated economists from a nearby university. Shortly after their arrival the two faculty members proposed the establishment of a center for public choice. University administrators approved the proposal, in part because they wanted to retain the recently recruited scholars and were afraid that denial of the request might signal their early departure.

The desire to strengthen graduate education programs and the research function also figures prominently in the willingness of administrators to establish institutes and centers. The bulk of university research funds and a significant proportion of the support for graduate students come from external sources, particularly the federal government. Interviews with administrators indicated that many of them believed, correctly or otherwise, that institutes could be more effective in generating needed external income for graduate education and research than could academic departments.

Much of the use of research centers to recruit and retain faculty members was aimed at strengthening graduate education and research programs. Staff members recruited and retained, in part, by institutes could and apparently did have considerable influence on graduate education programs, not only through their direct impact on strengthening the curriculum and by teaching courses, but indirectly by providing research experiences and apprentice research training for both graduate students and junior faculty members.

A third major effort of administrators was to improve communication within their complex institutions and effect better coordination of programs. This concern was aptly demonstrated by the vice-president for academic affairs of a large Big Ten university who observed that his university was a kind of "slumbering giant." Faculty members in separate departments and colleges did not know each other. Visitors to the campus, individuals of potential interest to several departments, frequently departed unknown to all but a small group of faculty members in a single department. Access to research equipment was restricted because of a lack of communication and problems of coordination.

It is not unusual for several departments to be engaged individually in research in a general area. Yet because of a number of barriers, they may have little or no contact with each other. The potential for interdepartmental collaboration is reduced, and the risk of apparent waste, useless duplication of effort, and general confusion among sponsors is increased. Such concerns were frequently mentioned in connection with the establishment of water centers and centers for environmental studies.

Some have likened the university to a federation, composed of departments, divisions, colleges, professional schools, institutes, and centers, each going its own way and following its own interests

(Clark, 1963). Much of the strength of the university as well as much inefficiency and vulnerability result from this condition. Clearly, however, some university administrators have attempted to use institutes and centers as one means of preserving the strengths of this federated diversity among departments and individual faculty members while reducing the negative consequences through increased cross-departmental communication and coordination.

Administrators also cited conflict resolution as a reason for creating institutes. These units are so frequently charged with generating dispute that it is difficult to imagine them as effective in avoiding or resolving conflicts, yet they do serve this function at times. In one major university, for example, one of the science departments was in dire need of reform, but action could not get under way until the chairman, who had served the department well in its early years, was replaced. The answer was to create a special center —in this case a water resources research center—which, in addition to serving its own purposes, would provide an attractive position for the department chairman to move to and thus would resolve an otherwise difficult situation in the change of departmental leadership.

Institutes are sometimes created *within* academic departments and colleges to serve a similar purpose. The problem of having two strong academic personalities—only one of whom can serve as department chairman—is occasionally handled by creating a center which is relatively autonomous from day-to-day departmental controls. Demands for greater recognition and more resources for a particular specialty or function within a department or college may also be met by creating an institute.

Although the recruitment and retention of faculty, strengthened graduate education and research, improved communication and coordination, and management of conflict relate directly to sustaining present goals and programs of the university, administrators also use institutes to exercise administrative initiative. One of the frequently mentioned motives was the need for the university to address new goals and serve new constituencies. One university president commented to this effect and was asked why academic departments could not serve these purposes just as well as, and perhaps even better than, institutes and centers. He replied that there was no apparent reason, but his experience suggested they rarely did.

Opportunities for university administrators to influence the course of the institution are few. Power is frequently limited to persuasion or the ability to block action through the control of funds. The administrator may be capable of stopping programs in a sector of the university, but he has difficulty influencing its goals or stimulating new programs. The chance to establish a new organization, help shape its goals, influence the selection of its personnel, and review its proposed programs does allow the administrator to make a positive impact. Since this initiative in influencing university goals is, in practice, considerably restricted in the conventional departmental structure, institutes apparently provide an attractive option.

These new organizations are also used by administrators as instruments of academic reform. One vice-president for academic affairs became convinced of the need to strengthen various social science departments and, particularly, to increase their competence in international studies. He called together a faculty group, including some of the stronger and younger members of several departments, and asked for and received a proposal for an institute for international and intercultural studies. The aim of the institute was to strengthen the very departments involved in the creation of it.

In another instance, a southwestern university had produced more graduate degrees in a decade or so than in the previous seventy-five years. As a result of this rapid growth and shift in function, the university had several departments considered weak and inadequate for graduate education. Institutes were used as one mechanism for attacking this weakness. The Graduate Institute of Statistics, for example, stemmed from concern over the quality of graduate instruction in mathematics. The institute was established in the mid-1960s, with the director reporting directly to the dean of the graduate school. Its responsibility was to provide graduate instruction in mathematics as well as statistics. The university, in

23

effect, created a second department of mathematics and recruited a director and staff who otherwise would not have joined the existing department.

While several instances can be cited of apparently effective use of institutes in departmental reform and institutional change, such efforts have also contributed to the feelings of hostility and suspicion toward these centers by many faculty members, particularly department chairmen and deans.

Some small universities use institutes and centers as a mechanism for increasing, disproportionately and selectively, the scale of university investment in a particular area or areas. These institutions of limited resources face obstacles as they attempt to compete with larger, better financed institutions. An institution with an enrollment of twelve thousand, for example, does not normally generate the same departmental strength in terms of numbers of faculty, depth and range of specialization, sophistication in research equipment, numbers of graduate students, and other factors as does a university with an enrollment and resources two or three times that size. The critical mass or the economies of scale of the large institution may not be available, but ambitions for academic greatness may nonetheless exist.

As an administrator of a small northeastern university pointed out, "The primary contribution of institutes and centers on this campus has been to enable us, as a small university in a comparatively small state, to select certain specific areas of excellence in which to increase our scale of operation and attract larger numbers of faculty than could otherwise have been possible." He went on to say that this disproportionate investment in a particular area could not have been justified on the basis of numbers of students alone but needed to be viewed as a mechanism for institutional development.

A border state university of comparable size wished to strengthen the social sciences in general and economics in particular. With the aid of a foundation grant, the university established a regional research institute and employed an economist with a national reputation as director. Although care was exercised to

24

keep the institute separate, and for the most part autonomous, from the department of economics, the net effect was to selectively transform that sector of the university. The department was able to attract faculty of a caliber that would have been impossible earlier because bright young staff members could obtain joint appointments in the institute, enjoy reduced teaching loads, and work with a scholar of national reputation. Graduate students gained research experience that had been unavailable. Although the social sciences were not greatly strengthened as a whole, the university substantially improved its position in economics.

Institutional visibility and prestige are difficult to define in the academic world and even more difficult to defend. Institutions of higher learning continue to rely disproportionately on apparent excellence, as measured, for example, by the Cartter report (1966), and on evidence of research productivity. For some universities the problem is to sustain and expand the recognized areas of excellence. For others, the task is to gain, for the first time, some small measure of recognition, even if only in one or two areas.

A selection of responses from administrators gives some of the flavor of their perceptions of past successes and future aspirations: "The primary contribution . . . has been to grasp a given area and really bring the program forward." "Institutes have helped . . . build our reputation as a real university." "The main effect has been to give increased visibility to certain program areas that will cause outsiders to look twice at us." "The main contribution has been the stimulation of a great deal of research."

A university graduate dean's comments, in a report to his faculty, illustrate the underlying concern of some university administrators:

> *To give focus and thrust to their research efforts, the* best schools [emphasis ours] *have established many of these units (institutes and centers), some having as many as 150. At our institution they have been largely neglected. . . . It roils me, as I believe it roils many of you, that we are not yet accepted as one of the now forty-six members of the Ameri-*

can Association of Universities. It disturbs me that in the Cartter report we have no departments listed as distinguished, no departments listed as strong, only three departments listed as good, and eight listed as adequate plus. When someone else mentions these points to me, I am quick to call attention to the fact that the evaluations are subjective and loaded with a particular kind of bias. But within the privacy of this group I shall admit that we have room for improvement.

No doubt this graduate dean and several other university administrators saw in institutes and centers the potential for realizing their hopes for institutional visibility, prestige, and recognition. Whether these organizations achieved those ends is an entirely different question.

Summary and Conclusions

Several forces largely external to universities have led them to modify their organizational structures. Recognition that research was not only useful but perhaps essential to progress in this scientifically and technologically advanced age and the dramatic increase in governmental and other support for university-based research changed the character of the university by changing its functions. Although support for research has slowed after the exuberant sixties, the long-term expectation that univerities will generate new knowledge and help accomplish social goals has not been reversed.

Changing societal needs and the growth of organized research in universities were accompanied by the expectation of sponsors that efforts would be task-oriented rather than discipline-oriented. The task, in turn, frequently required cross-disciplinary collaboration of individuals and a different organizational environment which maximized coordination and offered less professional autonomy than did the typical academic department.

These pressures for change came largely from agencies outside the university, and each contributed in a very fundamental way to the emergence of institutes and centers. The history of higher education is replete with illustrations of the impact of broad societal forces in shaping and changing colleges and universities. An understanding of institutes must certainly begin with an acknowledgment of these external pressures, but forces within institutions also played important roles. Career needs of faculty members and the concerns of university administrators for institutional development also contributed quite substantially to the proliferation of institutes and centers. Accounts of their origins in this study reveal that a majority stemmed from the initiative of a faculty member or group of faculty. University administrators reported selected cases in which faculty pressed relentlessly for the establishment of a center until the administration and grantor finally agreed.

Such faculty interest and pressure do not mean that a majority of the faculty favored establishing a given institute. It is increasingly unusual to find an instance in which a majority of faculty members approve any single proposal, including one for the creation of a center. In most cases their sanction is neither sought nor present. The essential element is rather the existence of a critical mass of faculty members led by a strong scholar-entrepreneur who can articulate the need for the institute, its goals, and the means available to achieve those ends, and who can mobilize the necessary support within and outside the university.

Analysis of institute origins, however, suggests strong influences from administrators. Institutes are used to help recruit and retain faculty members, solve problems of coordination and communication, strengthen graduate education and research programs, and resolve internal conflicts. Institutes are also used to enable the institution to address new goals, reform existing departments, establish special areas of academic emphasis, and enhance prestige.

Some degree of support from all three sectors—external constituent groups, the faculty, and university administrators—was usually present in the formation of an institute or center. To be sure, the importance of any given force tended to vary among institutes and among institutions. In some places, initiative came almost exclusively from the faculty, while in others it seemed to rest with members of the administration. Action was usually derived from a commitment to address a significant societal need; it received at least minimum concurrence from university administrators; and it enjoyed advocacy by a small group of concerned faculty members.

III

Structure

Some bemoan the existence of large, monolithic institutes, apparently independent of institutional controls, with separate staffs, lavish facilities, sizable budgets and questionable purposes. Others complain that institutes are too frequently "paper" organizations, figments of someone's imagination, with no apparent staff, no identifiable space or budget, and no apparent mission.

The answer to the apparent inconsistencies in perception, of course, is that fundamentally different organizations operate under the same names—institutes and centers. Many of these units do not have the characteristics we have come to expect in an *organization*. In some cases, for example, professional staff members devote or expect to devote the bulk of their careers to the center, while in others professional staff members remain full time in their departments, with no knowledge that a center pays a portion of their salary.

Direction of the Differences

Directors responded to three questions, the answers to which are helpful in the search for organizational differences among institutes and centers and between these organizations and academic departments. The questions were: (1) Are most of the professional staff members of the center officed in their respective

29

academic departments, rather than in the offices of your institute or center? (2) Are most of the professional staff appointments to the center or institute understood to be on a temporary, short-term (a year or so) basis? (3) Do you estimate that most of your professional staff members in the research center or institute maintain their primary ties and identification with their academic departments rather than with the center or institute?

Our intent was to tap the extent of organizational stability and the depth of staff identification with the institute or center. We assumed that an organization whose professional staff members viewed their appointments as temporary or of short duration, maintained offices elsewhere, and had primary ties and identification outside the unit was clearly different from the typical organization that housed its staff centrally, attempted to maximize staff stability, and was able to maintain staff loyalty to that organization, not others.

Responses to the three questions did turn out to be highly interrelated. As shown in Table 1, centers in which most professional staff members had their offices in their academic departments also tended to report that professional staff maintained their primary ties and identification with their academic departments.

A similar relationship was observed between the director's report of office locations and his view of staff appointments as

Table 1

OFFICE LOCATION AND PRIMARY TIES OF PROFESSIONAL STAFF

	Primary Ties in Department		Primary Ties outside Department		N.A.		Total
Offices in Department	65	(97%)	1	(2%)	1	(2%)	67
Offices in Institute	17	(31%)	37	(67%)	1	(2%)	55
Total	82	(67%)	38	(31%)	2	(2%)	122*

* Answers were received from 122 of 125 centers.

temporary, as reported in Table 2. As one would expect, a high proportion, 91 per cent of the centers in which most staff members were officed centrally also reported that staff appointments were *not* generally viewed as short-term or temporary in nature.

Table 2

OFFICE LOCATION AND EXPECTED DURATION OF APPOINTMENTS

	Appointments Viewed as Temporary		Appointments Not Viewed as Temporary		N.A.		Total
Offices in Department	38	(57%)	24	(36%)	5	(8%)	67
Offices in Institute	5	(9%)	50	(91%)			55
Total	43	(35%)	74	(61%)	5	(4%)	122

Centers that reported the bulk of staff offices were in academic departments also tended to acknowledge principal staff ties to the department, but centers that reported most staff offices were in the center did not necessarily claim that professional staff held their primary ties in the center. Similarly, centers that reported centralized staff offices tended to view staff appointments as more permanent, but the reverse did not necessarily hold true.

The relationship between the expected duration of appointments and primary ties and loyalty of staff members followed similar patterns. Responses reported in Table 3 indicate that center directors who viewed staff appointments as being short or temporary also believed by a seven-to-one margin that professional staff ties remained primarily with their academic departments. Again, however, the reverse did not necessarily hold true. Fifty-three per cent of those directors who reported that professional staff appointments were *not* viewed as short-term or temporary also believed that their staff members nonetheless maintained their primary ties and identification with their academic departments.

Of the total group of 125 institutes and centers, more than half reported that most of their staff members were housed in their

Table 3

EXPECTED DURATION OF APPOINTMENTS AND PRIMARY TIES
OF PROFESSIONAL STAFF

	Primary Ties in Department	Primary Ties Outside Department	N.A.	Total
Appointments Viewed as Temporary	38 (86%)	5 (11%)	1 (2%)	44 (37%)
Appointments Not Viewed as Temporary	40 (53%)	35 (46%)	1 (1%)	76 (63%)
Total	78 (65%)	40 (33%)	2 (2%)	120 (100%)

academic departments. Two-thirds of the directors reported that most professional staff members maintained their primary professional ties with their academic departments. And, more than a third—35 per cent—reported that appointments were understood to be temporary.

Apparent differences among institutes in different areas of concentration were identified (Table 4). Institutes in the physical-life sciences, for example, seemed to conform to the standard organizational expectations more closely. Over half the directors of these institutes indicated that staff members had their strongest ties with the center, not the department; nearly all indicated that appointments were not viewed as temporary; and most (75 per cent) reported that staff members were officed in the institute or center, not departments.

The interrelatedness of office location, duration of appointments, and primary staff ties and loyalties suggested a pattern of organizational types among institutes and centers. Two contrasting extremes emerged. The first is an institute with a centrally officed staff, employed on a continuing basis, whose primary ties are with the organization. The second has a professional staff employed on a short-term, temporary basis, with offices as well as professional ties and loyalties elsewhere. The first type of structure is character-

32

Structure

Table 4

OFFICE LOCATION, STAFF TIES, AND APPOINTMENT DURATION
IN THREE TYPES OF CENTERS

	Water Centers		Social Science Institutes		Physical-Life Science Institutes	
Are Professional Staff Housed in Their Academic Departments?						
Yes	44	(88%)	15	(35%)	8	(25%)
No	6	(12%)	25	(58%)	24	(75%)
Are Professional Staff Appointments Temporary?						
Yes	27	(54%)	15	(35%)	2	(6%)
No	18	(36%)	28	(65%)	30	(94%)
Do Professional Staff Maintain Primary Ties with Departments?						
Yes	47	(94%)	23	(54%)	13	(41%)
No	3	(6%)	19	(44%)	18	(56%)

NOTE: Sometimes the percentage columns do not total 100. The respondent did not answer or felt that the question was not applicable for his institute.

istic of most academic departments. The second type contrasts sharply with the norms one expects to find in the typical organization but it nevertheless describes many institutes and centers. The dynamics of these differences are examined below.

Standard, Adaptive, and Shadow Institutes

A taxonomy for examining the organizational differences among institutes and centers was suggested in an article by Selwyn Becker and Gerald Gordon (1966). Their taxonomy is based on two variables: the extent to which resources are stored within the organization, and the degree to which procedures are specified (p. 321). These two conditions hinge on still a third important factor: the degree of stability in the specific goals pursued or the tasks carried out by the organization and the degree of stability in the resource requirements necessary to achieve those goals and tasks. Greater stability allows an organization to accumulate and

33

store resources and to develop stable procedures for their use. When related to institutes and centers, the question becomes: To what extent is there stability in the programs, projects, or services carried out and to what extent is it possible or practical to store within the institute or center the necessary resources? Resources include, under this definition, men, materials, equipment, and space, as well as financial resources.

Becker and Gordon defined three organizational models according to their taxonomy: complete bureaucracies; truncated bureaucracies; and enucleated bureaucracies. With some variation in terminology as well as in substance of concepts, a related taxonomy might be applied to the organizational variations adopted by institutes and centers: standard institutes; adaptive institutes; and shadow institutes.

A standard institute has sufficient stability in goals and resources to develop a full managerial hierarchy and a permanent professional staff; to invest in potentially expensive equipment essential to its tasks; and to justify a reasonably permanent allocation of space. The standard institute very much resembles the standard bureaucratic organization in society. It is also typical of the organization models applied in the university, including not only the various administrative and supporting units such as admissions, registration, and counseling services, but academic departments as well. In all such units, staff members usually establish their primary ties and maintain their principal career identification within the unit, be it institute or department. They do not view the relationship as temporary. And there is sufficient stability in goals and tasks as well as in budget to make such organizational qualities not only possible but desirable.

The computer center, found now on nearly all university campuses, represents an obvious example of the standard model. The tasks carried out, with some modest variation, are essentially the same, day in and day out. Tasks must be sufficiently stable to warrant the purchase or rental on a continuing basis of expensive equipment and the employment of skilled technical personnel. Efforts are made to minimize staff turnover and to enhance staff loyalty to the center. Stability in budget as well as stability in space is essential.

A second example, the Materials Research Laboratory, also illustrates the standard model. The Laboratory was founded in 1962, partially in response to the government's interest in funding certain aspects of materials research on university campuses. The great bulk of the financial resources of the Laboratory, which operates with an annual budget of approximately a million dollars, is supplied by the federal government. The Laboratory has a full-time professional staff of thirty-two individuals at the rank of assistant professor or above. A smaller number of professional staff members are employed on a part-time but regular and continuing basis.

Although several professional staff members hold joint appointments in academic departments, they have a strong and in some instances a primary loyalty to the Laboratory. The Laboratory does not exercise full control over salary increases and promotions, but it exercises stronger control over personnel matters than do most other centers and institutes on the campus. The Laboratory is housed in a recently erected building and has acquired substantial amounts of specialized equipment. It tends, in short, to store within the organization the human, material, and physical resources necessary to accomplish its tasks and is able to do so because the demand for its services is reasonably constant and the services performed are quite stable.

But stability in tasks and resources is not always possible. As universities have attempted to respond to new needs, serve new constituencies, and carry out new functions, the specific tasks and the resources to carry them out can change—radically and rapidly. The contract or project model adopted by the federal government and by foundations as the principal means of securing research services from universities has contributed to the instability in institutional mission and in turn has brought forth the need for different and more adaptive organizational forms.

Grantors, for example, frequently want to "buy" only a specific package or project and it is difficult to anticipate with accuracy the specific configuration of human and material resources necessary to accomplish the job. Moreover, the configuration needed for one project may not be appropriate, or even possible, for another. The scale of operations will vary as well, and the institute may operate with many professional and supporting staff members for a brief period, then sharply reduce activity and staff size, secure another major contract, and then return to the previous high level of operation.

Adaptive institutes undergo a continuous process of redefining their goals, initiating and terminating projects, securing and releasing staff: in short, adapting to a persistent instability. They are likely to have a reasonably strong managerial hierarchy but only a small nucleus of professional staff members with continuing (although not necessarily continuous) ties with the institute.

Pertinent examples are the centers for educational research and school services set up by colleges of education to provide research services to school systems and at the same time enhance research opportunities for faculty. Such centers are frequently headed by a director and retain only a small central staff. Much of the professional staff for a given project is drawn from the faculty of the college, depending on the specific nature of the problem. In one instance the configuration might require an educational psychologist and curriculum specialist, while another task might require specialists in school building design and finance. The center typically has a few offices of its own and does invest in certain kinds of basic equipment and materials, but most of the personnel on the payroll will not be officed at the center and most of the equipment and materials will not necessarily belong to the center.

Water resources centers also tend to resemble the adaptive organizational model. The water center typically has a full-time director and often a full-time associate director. A small core of full-time and part-time staff may well be employed on a continuing basis, but the bulk of the professional staff members are not likely to have any long-term career identification with the water center. Staff members come from several departments—the average is

36

around six—and the departments as well as the specific individuals within them tend to shift from term to term as water centers take on new projects, close out old ones, redefine their missions, and secure new resources. The influence of the director, external grantors, and advisory committees—not professional staff—was judged to be most important in determining what the center did.

Numerous illustrations of the adaptive institute can be found. Indeed, this type is the model against which many faculty members and administrators judge institutes and centers. Adaptive institutes are viable organizations with functions and resources, but they are not the large-scale, permanent bureaucracies characteristic of the standard model. They represent the middle ground designed to maintain flexibility in personnel commitments, space, equipment, and other resources sufficient to make major changes in the goals and tasks pursued as well as in the procedures followed.

Shadow institutes form the third category. Is an institute that has no staff, no space, no budget, and no visible accomplishments in fact an institute? One university vice-president commented that he read in the newspaper almost weekly about new institutes supposedly created on his campus, which, to his knowledge, had no legitimate or officially authorized status. They were, he pointed out, instruments of faculty fantasy. In the process of assembling centers for participation in this study, replies were received from directors of several apparent institutes who reported that no organization really existed. The puzzle was that it had been earlier claimed to exist.

Such shadow institutes typically have a designated director, but usually he is employed on only a part-time basis. He may devote none of his time to the institute for long periods. Typically, professional staff members, including the director, do not have strong ties to the institute. The shadow institute usually has no budget of its own, but it may exercise influence, if not some actual control, over other budgets in the university. In terms of space, the institute is hard to find. It has no single central location. The director's office is typically masked by another university unit and function such as that of graduate dean or department chairman.

Frequently, the headquarters of the shadow institute turns out to be a file drawer in the office of a faculty member.

Examples of the shadow model are institutes whose primary function is coordination and general surveillance of a particular institution-wide program or function. The Institute of Biological Sciences at one university is one. In its early stages, a vice-president served as director on a part-time basis. The institute had no budget of its own. The staff was composed entirely of faculty members in the biological science departments in the colleges of arts and sciences, agriculture, and medicine. In fact, the great majority of faculty members listed as members of the institute had no firsthand contact or other tangible relationship with it. The institute was nonetheless effective, in a limited way, in improving coordination and communication among several university departments, enabling the university to give higher budgetary priority to the biological sciences and providing a broader base for certain graduate education and research programs.

Shadow institutes, sometimes also called "paper" institutes, can provide a neutral ground on which faculty members from several departments can come together for initial small-scale collaboration in teaching and research. The institute has no substance, as such, but it apparently helps reduce apprehension and ease academic protocol so that faculty members with like interests can work more closely together. Many people wonder what is being accomplished through such an "institute" that could not be accomplished through more informal collaboration among faculty members and departments. The answer frequently turns out to be "little, if anything," but the obvious absence of such informal crossdepartmental collaboration on any significant scale in most universities has apparently convinced some that a few low-profile, low-budgeted, shadow institutes may be a good investment.

One of the more common shadow institutes is an institute which at one time carried out a rather sizable task but became dormant after finishing its project. Some argue that such units should be given a decent burial and eventually an official death certificate. As a practical matter of campus politics, however, institutes do not die that easily or quickly. More important, the dormant institute sometimes possesses a latent network of professional ties and contacts both within and beyond the campus that may be potentially useful. Although inactive, the institute could be strengthened and transformed into a more substantial organization should a legitimate need arise. In such cases, the costs of maintaining the institute must be weighed against the potential benefits of this added institutional capacity and flexibility.

Some shadow institutes perform other less laudable functions, including the provision of comfortable sinecures for faculty members and administrators the institution wishes to move out of the mainstream; the satisfaction of private and solely personal faculty ambitions; the luxury of faculty fantasy; and a means for institutional and self-deception. But as an organizational type, the shadow institute represents an interesting alternative to the conventional, highly structured, typically inflexible, and overly bureaucratic models of organization so characteristic of colleges and universities as well as other social institutions.

Summary and Conclusions

Three major organizational models of institutes and centers can be identified: standard, adaptive and shadow. The three models tended to fall along a single continuum and differ in terms of stability in goals and programs; duration of appointments; strength of identification of professional staff members with the institute; control over budget; and the manner in which space and facility needs are satisfied.

The standard institute model tends to resemble more closely the standard bureaucratic organization form. The adaptive and shadow models tend to depart from this norm with more flexible definitions of mission; ability to change procedures and programs more radically; a more extensive use of temporary, part-time professional staff appointments; the use of less conventional budgetary systems; and space requirements that can be met very largely through the use of borrowed and unassigned facilities. The result is a system of trade-offs, for certain advantages and benefits accrue from these organizational models, but their application brings still another set of problems.

The most obvious advantage of adaptive and shadow institutes is the added institutional flexibility in accepting new missions and in adapting to changing demands. The absence of a permanent professional staff is crucial, for the moment an institute or center settles on a permanent staff, it tends to restrict its mission to those things that this staff is competent and committed to do. Reliance on temporary appointments gives the institute greater continuing flexibility in staff capability and the chance to adapt the staff configuration to meet the task, rather than to define the task to fit staff competencies.

This greater flexibility can be translated into greater institutional responsiveness. While colleges and universities as well as other social institutions are frequently criticized for their failure to be sufficiently responsive to changing societal needs and conditions, the very organizational survival of the adaptive or shadow institute may depend on its responsiveness. Many directors complain that there is very little apparent institutional commitment to provide continuing financial support. As a result, they are forced to respond to the needs and wishes of particular sponsors outside the university. The direct link between many institutes and their external constituents is a high-risk endeavor, but for all its weaknesses, it nonetheless provides a more responsive connection between the university and society.

A third and little exploited advantage of the adaptive and shadow institute model is that it provides a more realistic organizational mechanism for the application of program planning and budgeting systems. Despite the apparent application of PPBS, most higher education program planning and budgeting remains largely incremental and unrelated to specific functions. Departments are not highly susceptible to change, especially if "change" means less money, space, equipment, or personnel this year than last year. While directors of so-called adaptive and shadow institutes do not welcome a budget cut any more than do other academic administrators, most have learned to manage in the face of wide fluctuations in resources, to accommodate the irregular initiation and termination of programs, and to accept the concept of program rather than incremental budgeting. The performance of institutes and centers along these lines might be strengthened further by greater recognition and legitimation of this advantage.

Adaptive and shadow institutes carry with them liabilities as well as assets. Shadow institutes are criticized, for example, because they do not conform to typical expectations as to what an organization should be. Perhaps for this reason and to achieve greater stability and reduce organizational strains, institute directors frequently attempt to push their institutes along the continuum. They tend to secure space, seek budgets, build permanent staffs, and seek stable missions. In the process, they are transformed from shadow or adaptive institutes into standard institutes. Grantors external to the university look for stability and permanence and are not impressed by apparent paper organizations. Grantors want to see and frequently press for greater institutional commitment.

Genuine problems of managerial strain are imposed by radical and rapid adaptation and change. Adaptive and shadow institutes tend to provide less career security, less opportunity for long-term identification with an organizational unit, and perhaps fewer personal satisfactions for staff members. Too little is known about such potential problems and even less about effective measures for resolving them. Certainly some of this strain could be reduced by increased institutional understanding.

Another liability is the hazard of goal displacement. The desire for survival runs strong in most organizations, and institutes and centers are no exception. Laudable qualities of adaptation and flexibility can become liabilities when the institute subverts the purpose defined in its original charter. Recent attention to defense-oriented research and to the conduct of classified research for industry as well as for the military has brought to light instances of apparent goal displacement, sometimes to the dismay not only of the institutes but of the institution as a whole. The "adaptability" of institutes and centers has gone largely unmonitored at many

41

universities and needs greater surveillance if the assets of flexibility are to be retained.

As a final note, accountability mechanisms must take a somewhat different form in the shadow or adaptive institute. Center directors, for example, have few controls over the system of faculty rewards and sanctions. They may not be able, for example, to ensure promotions, salary raises, and other rewards for superior staff performance. It is difficult at times to hold individuals accountable in an organization in which staff members are constantly changing and have their principal ties and loyalties elsewhere. Budget controls also can be more difficult to exercise if institute resources are fragmented in the budgets of several departments throughout the university.

Institutional accountability, on the other hand, can be strengthened. Realignment of the institutional structure along task-oriented lines allows stronger bonds between structure and function to be built. Thus, on balance, adaptive and shadow institutes may complicate the reward mechanisms for individual staff members yet increase the capacity of the organization itself to stand accountable for its performance.

IV

Functions

☙☙☙☙☙☙☙☙☙☙☙☙☙☙☙☙☙☙☙☙☙☙☙

Many functions are carried out by institutes, and the nature and combinations of these activities differ drastically. To complicate matters, there are sharp differences of opinion about what institutes ought to do. Some faculty, administrators, and institute staff believe that institutes ought to have essentially the same functions as departments but enjoy greater autonomy of operation, carry fewer teaching responsibilities, and report at higher levels in the university's organizational hierarchy. Others stress the multidisciplinary character as essential to understanding their functions. Institutes and centers, they note, might carry on the same functions of instruction, research, and public service as departments, but they differ from departments principally because of the several disciplines involved.

A third view emphasizes their applied rather than basic or theoretical orientation. Viewed in this way, institutes function "to solve the problems of men" (Smith, 1966) while basic research and theory-building are the tasks of departments. The application of knowledge and the solution of problems should be the aims of centers.

A somewhat cynical conception of the role of institutes is that of a profit-oriented, income-generating unit whose primary function is to sustain itself economically and, if possible, to "show a profit" that might be redirected to other sectors of the university.

Under this definition the director tends to be viewed as an entrepreneur and his success or failure is calculated primarily on the basis of the number and size of externally supported contracts, the amount of money made available for graduate student stipends, research support for faculty members, and, of course, the amount of overhead monies generated for reallocation throughout the system.

In a literal sense, none of these views is accurate. In a more general sense, each suggests the diversity and lack of clarity in institute activities. A more precise understanding is useful in several ways. Most important, perhaps, is that organizations tend to be evaluated in terms of function—the extent to which they achieve their goals. Inappropriate expectations and inaccurate assumptions are not likely to provide the best basis from which to evaluate performance.

The functions carried out by an institute influence to a considerable degree the characteristics of its organizational structure. Certain functions or combinations of them may require one set of characteristics while another configuration employs quite a different structure. Failure to understand variations in functions and to recognize the interrelationships between function and structure may lead to the adoption of inappropriate organizational models as well as inaccurate appraisals of existing organizational arrangements.

Interdisciplinary Collaboration

The special ability of institutes and centers to facilitate interdisciplinary collaboration is regarded by many as one of the prime justifications for their existence. This rationale implies that if the task were manageable by a single disciplinary group, it could and should be done within an academic department. Such an assumption, however, appears in conflict with the fact that the staff of many institutes comes predominantly from a single discipline or profession.

Several factors have contributed to the growing emphasis

on multidisciplinary research and teaching. The so-called knowledge explosion contributed to the fragmentation of disciplines into new and important specialties and to the emergence of new cross-disciplinary relationships. Prior to achieving recognized disciplinary status of its own, such crossdisciplinary collaboration is typically described as multi- or interdisciplinary. It may remain multidisciplinary in character, or it may turn out to be the breeding ground for a new "discipline." In either case, the institute or center may prove useful as an incubator in which the infant can be conceived, nourished, and developed. Thus, from one perspective, such institutes can be viewed as interdisciplinary, but from another they are highly specialized in their disciplinary orientation.

The second major push toward interdisciplinary collaboration has been the increased demand for applied knowledge to solve scientific, technical, and social problems. Problem-solving cannot necessarily be restricted to disciplinary boundaries. Those who sponsor problem-solving research and development in universities tend to give highest priority to the accomplishment of their tasks and are typically less interested in the advancement of the discipline, *per se*. Jencks and Riesman (1968) point out that the clash between the interests and motives of sponsors and those of faculty members is not as intense as might be imagined, because academicians are less particular about the areas in which they work, so long as they are free to choose their methods. And sponsors have few preconceptions about methods, so long as they can control the problem focus of the investigation (p. 516).

Directors in the study were asked to indicate the *nature* of their interdisciplinary involvement and the extent of interdisciplinary collaboration in their institutes. Three different modes of collaboration were identified. Staff members from different disciplines, for example, may work together as a team on a single project. They may design the study together, carry out the research as a team, and write a single, integrated report of their findings.

Although the second model also involves staff members from different disciplines, individuals tend to work independently on separate aspects of a larger problem. There may be an overall, integrative design to the total enterprise, but substantial autonomy is granted each of the investigators in the design and direction of separate phases of the effort.

A third model, though sometimes described as interdisciplinary, actually involves faculty members primarily from a single discipline. The backgrounds of the researchers, the methodology, and the definition of the problem reflect the dominance of a single discipline or professional area. The model is distinguished from conventional departmental research in that it has a task orientation, and personnel from outside the discipline or professional area may join the research effort as required on a supporting basis. A program of research and development operated by engineers, for example, may also require the services of a sociologist; a team of physicists may need the support of a biologist; or an institute of educational research may need the expertness of a psychologist or an economist.

Directors were asked to indicate which of the above types best described the nature of interdisciplinary collaboration in their institute or center. Their responses are reported in Table 5.

Table 5

NATURE OF INTERDISCIPLINARY INVOLVEMENT

Nature of Collaboration	Water Centers		Social Science Institutes		Physical-Life Science Institutes	
Integrated collaboration	18	(36%)	14	(33%)	17	(53%)
Independent projects	20	(40%)	8	(19%)	7	(22%)
Single discipline dominance	9	(18%)	10	(23%)	7	(22%)
Little inter-disciplinary involvement	3	(6%)	11	(26%)	1	(3%)
Total	50	(100%)	43	(101%)	32	(100%)

Functions

Most interdisciplinary activity in water centers fell into the second category of involvement, that is, independent projects which were part of a larger design. Forty per cent of the directors indicated this mode as most descriptive of the collaboration in their centers. An additional 36 per cent of the directors designated integrated interdisciplinary collaboration as most characteristic of the work in their center. Single disciplinary involvement with support from other disciplines as needed was named by only 18 per cent of the water center directors.

Responses from the directors of physical-life science institutes revealed a similar pattern, except that integrated interdisciplinary collaboration was ranked higher (53 per cent) than independent projects (22 per cent). The single discipline model again ranked third (22 per cent), and, as with water center directors, only a minor fraction of the directors indicated little or no interdisciplinary involvement.

The situation in the social sciences was different, however, and suggested a somewhat weaker interdisciplinary emphasis. Although 33 per cent of directors called integrated work most characteristic, approximately one-quarter of the directors indicated little or no interdisciplinary involvement and an additional 23 per cent indicated the predominance of the single-discipline model in which other disciplines were used principally for supporting purposes.

The extent of interdisciplinary involvement, irrespective of form, was also explored, and the results are reported in Table 6. Were all projects interdisciplinary in nature, or if not all, could most projects be so classified? Thirty per cent of the water center directors reported that most projects were interdisciplinary, but the majority (58 per cent) reported some interdisciplinary emphasis in selected projects. Only a small fraction of water center directors responded in the extremes.

Directors of institutes in the physical-life sciences reported a somewhat stronger interdisciplinary emphasis: one-quarter claimed heavy interdisciplinary involvement in nearly all projects. An additional third reported interdisciplinary emphasis in most projects.

47

Table 6

EXTENT OF INTERDISCIPLINARY INVOLVEMENT

Extent of Involvement	Water Centers		Social Science Institutes		Physical-Life Science Institutes	
Heavy, in nearly all projects	2	(4%)	6	(14%)	8	(25%)
Emphasis in most projects	15	(30%)	12	(28%)	11	(34%)
Some emphasis selected projects	29	(58%)	16	(37%)	9	(28%)
Work within disciplinary lines	4	(8%)	9	(21%)	4	(13%)
Total	50	(100%)	43	(100%)	32	(100%)

The major difference in the extent of interdisciplinary activity was again apparent among institutes and centers in the social sciences. One-fifth (21 per cent) of their directors reported essentially no interdisciplinary emphasis. The modal response was "some interdisciplinary emphasis in selected projects." Social science institutes were also characterized by a wide range in responses. Fourteen per cent of the directors reported a heavy interdisciplinary emphasis in nearly all projects and an additional 21 per cent indicated that most of their institute's work was conducted within disciplinary lines.

Interdisciplinary activity can also be assessed by examining the number of different departments or disciplines represented on the institute staff. The data in Table 7 suggest a picture somewhat at variance with directors' reports of interdisciplinary activity. Forty-two per cent of the social science units and 38 per cent of the physical-life science institutes showed two or fewer departments represented. By contrast, more than one-quarter of the water center directors reported at least ten academic departments or disciplines. The heavier crossdepartmental representation shown by water center staffs can be explained in part by the nature of their missions and also by the character of their organizational structure, a point covered later in greater detail.

Table 7

NUMBER OF ACADEMIC DEPARTMENTS REPRESENTED ON
INSTITUTE STAFFS

Number of Departments	Water Centers		Social Science Institutes		Physical-Life Science Institutes	
0 to 2	3	(6%)	18	(42%)	12	(38%)
3 to 6	9	(18%)	18	(42%)	7	(22%)
7 to 10	25	(50%)	4	(9%)	10	(31%)
10 or more	13	(26%)	3	(7%)	3	(9%)
Total	50	(100%)	43	(100%)	32	(100%)

The comparatively small number of departments or disciplines represented in other institutes and centers calls into question certain director reports of strong interdisciplinary emphasis. Perhaps the function of interdisciplinary research has been over-emphasized as a justification for institutes. These figures also suggest that definitions of what is disciplinary and what is inter-disciplinary may differ considerably among centers and more generally in the academic world. Such data in no way invalidate interdisciplinary collaboration as a factor in the creation of centers, but they do suggest that collaboration may be only one of several forces and functions—and, at least in some institutes, a compara-tively minor one at that.

Research, Public Service, and Teaching

Two indicators were used to identify functions carried out by institutes included in this study. We analyzed the directors' brief written descriptions of the essential mission of their center; and we examined the estimated distribution of center resources among the functions of research, public service, and instruction.

Analysis of the directors' statements indicated that research and public service were the primary or predominant functions. Of the forty-three social science centers included, for example, approximately one-quarter emphasized research as their sole function while some 12 per cent identified public service as their sole function. An additional one-third indicated combined functions of research and public service. No social science institute indicated instruction as its sole function, and instruction was mentioned in combination with other functions by only about one-fourth of the social science units.

A slightly different pattern emerged for institutes in the physical and life sciences. Nearly half, 47 per cent, described research as their sole function, while an additional one-fourth mentioned combined functions of research and teaching. Only two of the thirty-two physical and life science units stressed instruction as their primary or sole function. Water center director responses tended to resemble the physical-life science pattern most closely with considerably more emphasis on the administration and coordination of research and public service functions.

Centers apparently allocated their time and resources roughly in accord with their statements of mission. Each director was asked to estimate the approximate distribution of resources among the functions of research, public service, and instruction. These estimates suggested patterns similar to the earlier reports of mission, as shown in Figure 1.

Research is of primal importance in all three categories, with noticeable variations. Water centers, on the average, devoted more than 80 per cent of their resources to research. Two-thirds of the resources of physical-life science institutes were devoted to research, but a surprising one-quarter of their resources was devoted to the instructional function. In contrast, the social science-humanities units apportioned 26 per cent of their resources to public service functions, a much higher proportion than that for the other two groups. Some social science units were principally devoted to the public service function, but no water center or physical-life science center devoted more than 50 per cent of its time to public service, and an allocation of considerably less than

Functions

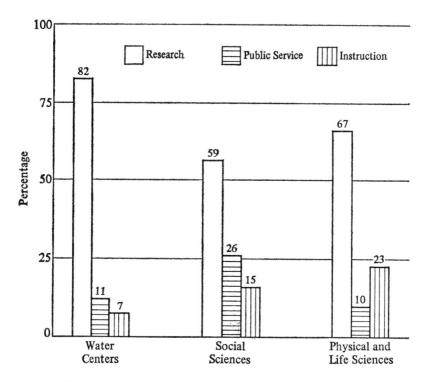

FIGURE 1. Distribution of center resources among functions.

20 per cent of institute resources to public service functions was more typical.

The distribution of resources among functions is somewhat predictable. Many water centers are functionally and structurally organized for research only. By contrast, the social science-humanities groupings gave evidence of their service orientation in units such as bureaus of business and economic research, institutes of government and public affairs, or institutes of public administration. These units were created in large part as an aid to business and public officials, to keep them abreast of current developments, to provide pertinent social, economic, or political data, and to train or retrain practitioners for service in the public sector .

Since most centers and institutes are prohibited from offering degree programs, the emphasis on instruction suggested by physical-life science institute directors was surprising. In terms of scale of operations as reflected by budgets and staffing, these centers far outdistanced the others. Most institute directors reported graduate students associated with their centers, but the physical-life science institutes clearly ranked highest in this regard. They also employed an appreciable number of postdoctoral fellows.

Performance, Facilitation, and Administration

The way in which institutes and centers pursue the tasks of instruction, research, and public service may be more significant than the functions themselves. Institutes, for example, may attempt to perform their functions directly; they may work to facilitate the performance of others; or they may elect to administer or manage the process whereby the functions are performed. These alternative approaches are thus important to an understanding of the distinctive functioning of institutes. The interaction of the three task areas (research, public service, and instruction) with the three principal means of approaching these tasks (performance, facilitation, and administration) provides the framework for examining variation in function.

Performance of research. The direct conduct of research by a relatively stable professional staff is perhaps the most common stereotype of what institutes are all about. The following brief description of a physics laboratory provides a useful example of an institute whose principal function is research performance. Founded in 1945 through the joint efforts of the university administration and the Office of Naval Research, the laboratory conducts research in high energy, nuclear, and cosmic ray physics. It was budgeted at more than three million dollars in 1969 although the university's contribution amounted to less than 15 per cent of the total. All fifty professional persons employed by the unit are paid in part or full from the laboratory's funds and represent only one academic discipline, physics. Administratively, the laboratory is under the aegis of the physics department.

Facilitation of research. Not all institutes and centers, however, perform research. Rossi (1964), for example, correctly points out that "the first research center to evolve within the structure of the university was the library, occurring at a stage so deep in the beginnings of the institution that we usually do not classify the library as a center for research" (p. 1143). Its more recent counterparts—the computer center and the nuclear reactor laboratory, for example—have emerged on many campuses and are designed to facilitate research, not necessarily to produce it. They do so through providing facilities, services, consultation, materials, and other resources essential to the conduct of research.

The Plant Environmental Laboratory, established in 1967 by a southeastern univeristy to provide climate-control laboratories and to assist faculty members at that institution and at other universities throughout the southeast in their research, provides a good illustration of an institute which facilitates research. The laboratory was brought into being through the efforts of several faculty members from the college of agriculture and has no professional staff of its own other than a part-time director from the botany faculty. A small staff of skilled technicians operates the laboratory and maintains the controlled environment essential for certain plant studies.

A second and less obvious example is a Human Resources Research Institute. The institute was established in 1965 as part of a larger effort to upgrade the graduate instruction and research programs in education and social work of a middle-sized university. The principal purpose of the institute was to enhance the research productivity of the college as a whole, and it attempted to do so by providing statistical and research design consultation assistance, making available research equipment, providing released time for research for selected faculty members, and helping move good research ideas into proposal form. Although the institute was established to facilitate and not to produce research, there was a strong tendency for its professional staff members to want to shift the function toward research production and for those outside the institute to appraise its performance in terms of the actual production of research, not its facilitation.

Beyond Academic Departments

Administration of research. Administration has never been among the more popular functions of the university, and few institutes and centers actually think of administration or the management of research as their principal function. Many institutes, however, are primarily administrative units that assemble and coordinate a variety of resources including materials, space, equipment, time, and, of course, people, toward the achievement of a single research task.

Perhaps the national network of water centers provides the best example of institutes designed to administer research. Research programs on the problems of water quantity and quality may require competencies from several disciplines, and as problems shift over time, the specific professional talent, equipment, and facilities required also change. An economist, rural sociologist, chemist, or biologist may be essential at one point but not needed at another. As a result, most water centers employ staff members from several departments, most of whom maintain their principal identification with their departments. The task of maintaining and coordinating these complex interpersonal and organizational relationships is considerable.

It is therefore not by accident that approximately half of the fifty water center directors stressed the center's role in administration and coordination of research. Although all water centers are administratively responsible for the research carried out under their sponsorship, much of this research is actually "produced" in the various academic departments throughout the university. The principal task, then, is to coordinate efforts and ensure accountability to sponsors.

The function of some institutes is even more administrative in nature. Some research centers have responsibility for administering and overseeing the conduct of sponsored research in a broad, general area. The Center for Research of the College of Business in a large eastern university represents an attempt to centralize the administration of sponsored research in that college. The center aids college faculty members in securing research support and exercises administrative and budget controls.

Functions

The significant point is not so much the classification as a producer, facilitator, or administrator of research, but the recognition that this variety is present. This diversity and functional differentiation make the institute or center a useful organizational alternative in the complex university.

Performance of public service. The Agricultural Extension Service represents the oldest, best established, and most obvious example of an institute which produces public service in land-grant universities. Another example is the Center for Industrial Research and Service, established in 1963 at a midwestern institution, which provides direct delivery of public service. The impetus for the center came from the state's industrial leaders, with the dean of engineering acting as the intermediary in presenting their needs to the university administration and board of regents. Because of the past tradition of service to agriculture by the Cooperative Extension Division, the Center for Industrial Research consciously patterned itself after the agriculture model. In the general description of the center's mission, the director stated that the center offered guidance and technical advice to the state's industrial firms on problems of management, production, marketing, organization, and sales. Eighteen professionals representing twelve disciplines comprise the center's personnel, and despite its "business orientation," more than 75 per cent of the center's financial support is provided by the university.

Facilitation of public service. Though no institute in our study had the principal function of facilitating public service, conference centers maintained by many universities, for example, have been established to facilitate delivery of public service, not to provide it directly. Typically, a central management staff operates or secures facilities in which conferences, seminars, workshops, and other continuing education and public service activities can take place.

Administration of public service. Offices or divisions of continuing education are not typically regarded as institutes and centers on most campuses, and yet they are, in essence, task-oriented mechanisms designed to administer the delivery of public services.

Such units assemble information on continuing education needs, identify and coordinate university talent and resources necessary to meet the needs, but typically they do not provide the service themselves. Their primary function is to coordinate its delivery.

Many institutes of public administration and public affairs bureaus approximate the public-service administration model. Along with assembling talent and resources from the university at large, the personnel associated with these units usually also maintain a professional interest in the services offered. One illustration is a Bureau of Public Affairs Research established in 1959 at a small university in the West. Its director reported that the highest priorities of the bureau are to: (1) provide administrative research materials and facilities for city, county, and state officials as well as the university faculty and students; and (2) offer short courses, institutes, and other training activities for mayors and councilmen, city clerks and treasurers, county officials, state legislative budget staff, and local law-enforcement administrators. There is only one full-time professional staff member, a political scientist. The associate director is an economist and former state budget director. Along with representatives from other disciplines, these two attempt to coordinate the delivery of the institution's expertise to state and local governments.

Production of instruction. As a general rule, academic departments exercise rather carefully guarded property rights in the direct delivery of instructional services. Either by policy regulation or by informal understanding, most universities prohibit institutes and centers from offering courses and providing instructional services unless it is done in cooperation with and under the auspices of an academic department. However, there are exceptional cases in which the institute or center functions and is treated as if it were, in fact, an academic department. The Center for the Study of Higher Education at the University of Michigan, for example, performs the full range of instructional, research, and public service functions characteristic of an academic department.

The Near Eastern Center established in 1957 at a university on the West Coast provides a useful example of a center in which the conduct of instruction is the primary function. Language instruction is handled through the conventional academic departments, but the center provides research and training facilities which integrate language skills with all dimensions of the Middle Eastern culture. Unlike many centers of this genre, the Near Eastern Center grants an interdisciplinary degree in Islamic Studies.

The more significant instruction provided by most institutes and centers takes the indirect form of research apprenticeship experiences for graduate students and junior faculty members. Although most of this instruction frequently goes unrecognized in terms of credits, grades, or courses, it is nonetheless important. Rossi (1964), for example, has observed that tensions between academic departments and research institutes are sometimes exacerbated when graduate students employed in an institute are taught and use research methodologies that their professors find foreign and are unable to follow (p. 1154). Typically, however, such tensions are kept within manageable limits, and the provision of research apprentice experience is generally viewed on all sides as a very useful, even though indirect, function.

Facilitation of instruction. Some assert that the sole justification for institutes and for the sponsored research they carry out is to facilitate and strengthen graduate education. One university administrator, hearing that several centers on his campus were supposedly engaged only in the conduct of research, took issue with the claim. In his view, all research units on the campus should contribute to and facilitate the graduate programs of the university, and if they failed to meet this test, they did not belong on the campus.

Institutes do facilitate graduate education programs by providing employment for graduate students, but there are very real differences among institutes in this regard. Nearly all water centers, for example, employed some graduate students as research assistants or research associates. Over half of the water centers reported having ten or more graduate students employed and 38 per cent reported twenty or more graduate students as staff members. A similar pattern was identified for institutes and centers in the physical and natural sciences. Half of these units employed ten or more graduate students and 12 per cent employed fifty or more graduate students.

Social science units reflect a different pattern. Thirty per cent reported no graduate students employed and an additional 49 per cent indicated that fewer than ten graduate students were working in their centers. Such contrasts may reflect a different scale of operation for social science centers, which tend to be smaller. Perhaps the data also reflect different attitudes in the social sciences toward the appropriate role of institutes in facilitating graduate instruction. Another possibility is that evidence of graduate student participation in a proposed research program in the physical or natural sciences may be essential to its approval by a funding agency, while inclusion of a graduate assistant in the budget of a research proposal in the social sciences may require more careful documentation of the student's role and his anticipated contribution to the project. Whatever the cause, apparent differences in the relationship between institutes and graduate education were identified among broad disciplinary areas.

Administration of instruction. One of the most common functions of institutes heavily engaged in instruction is administration and coordination in a specific area that involves faculty members and resources from several academic departments. A genetics institute established in 1958 by a medium-sized university is a case in point. The university found that geneticists were located in several departments throughout the university but their efforts were fragmented and frequently duplicative. By forming an institute, managed by a three-man executive committee, the university was able to pool its modest resources, increase the depth and scale of its graduate program in genetics, and do so without a significant cost increase.

Certain Latin American, Far Eastern, African, Caribbean, Spanish, Russian, and Chinese "area studies" centers administer or coordinate instruction. Under such a model, faculty members typically retain their primary identification with their academic departments, but they may also be "members" of or hold an appointment in the center. The institute may or may not have a budget of its own and may have very little by way of a central facility. To accomplish its mission, the center needs legitimacy as the spokesman for the "area," a coordinating mechanism of some sort either in the form of a director or an executive committee, and the cooperation of the academic departments and faculty members involved.

Though this study focuses specifically on research institutes, it should be apparent that institutes can reform, facilitate, or administer all university functions. The significance lies less in the nine types of functions suggested above than in the limitations placed on their activities. Few institutes are restricted to only one of the nine categories. Most define their mission around a combination of functions, such as the performance of research and the facilitation of instruction. The mandate is nonetheless much less broad than that of the typical academic department.

As universities have taken on more functions and have increased their research and public service activities, the organizational structure has remained essentially the same. The bulk of the added burden has been carried by expanding the functions of departments and enlarging the performance expectations of faculty members. Not only has there been no limit placed on legitimate departmental functions, there has been a clear expectation that departments should carry out the full range of the university's activities and that faculty performance should be judged against the same comprehensive scale.

The usefulness of institutes and centers lies, in large part, in providing an organizational alternative. By restricting the principal mission to one or two functions (research, instruction, or public service) and perhaps only one or two principal approaches to addressing that function (facilitation, administration, or performance), institutes enable greater task specialization, more direct relationships among programs, budgets, and organizational structure, and greater organizational capability in meeting specific needs.

Summary and Conclusions

It is interesting to speculate about why the claims of interdisciplinary involvement in institutes tend to outrun the actual evidence. Department chairmen and departmental faculties usually retain control of many important rewards and sanctions, including the award of professorial rank, recommendations for promotion, and grants of tenure. Pleasing departments is an important matter for most institute directors, and it may be easier to build and maintain close relationships with two departments than to attempt to please a dozen.

It is also possible that institutes may tend to take on a disciplinary bias in spite of best intentions. Mores and values in personnel selection may cause professional staff members to value candidates with views and competencies in harmony with their own, and thus the institutes may evolve a more homogeneous staff over time. Different disciplines define the same problem differently and tend to approach tasks with different methodological tools and procedures. The process of defining tasks and resolving these "differences" very likely screens in certain disciplines and screens out others. In short, one could hypothesize that the same forces which have escalated the power and attractiveness of academic departments in recent decades have exerted a continuing pressure toward disciplinary homogeneity in institutes and centers as well.

The critical functional aspect may not be the number of departments involved but the adoption of a task orientation rather than a disciplinary orientation. This can, of course, take place with one or twenty disciplines involved. The involvement of several disciplines does not ensure the accomplishment of a task or the solution of a problem and may only indicate a splintering of resources among several disciplines.

Interdisciplinary collaboration is only one of several functions institutes perform. Much of the confusion about institutes stems from the wide variety of activities they carry out. In contrast to the academic department, which typically has few if any restrictions placed on its role, most institutes are limited principally to a few specific functions such as the performance of research, the administration of public service, or the facilitation of instruction, while carrying out other actions on a more informal, supplementary basis. Institute directors and staff members sometimes complain about restrictions placed on their goals and functions and would prefer a broader and more general mandate. A wider range of functions, teaching as well as research, allows them to satisfy more personal and professional needs. Even though employed full time in a research capacity, for example, institute staff members frequently volunteer to teach classes without extra remuneration. Related to this issue is the belief that institutes with broader mandates have greater recruitment appeal. A synergetic argument of long standing in colleges and universities is also advanced, suggesting that ideas generated in one activity, say research, stimulate improved performance in another activity, for example teaching.

Over a third of the water center directors indicated that their centers should embrace research, public service, and instruction. Even a larger proportion of the social science and humanities institute directors, nearly one-half, indicated that their centers should be allowed to perform all three. The heaviest push toward multifunctional status, however, was evidenced by the physical and life science institutes; fully 75 per cent of the directors believed that their institute *should* conduct all three activities.

There are pros and cons involved, but considering the overall configuration of the university, attempts to expand institutes to a multifunctional status would be unfortunate. Such expansion would tend, over time, to minimize the unique functional advantages of centers as an alternative organizational form. The present, more restricted mission and task orientation of institutes allows them to meet specific needs more efficiently and effectively and with greater flexibility than is possible in many academic departments, schools, or colleges. If their functions were expanded to include responsibilities for the full range of university activities, and if limitations on their missions were removed, they would become indistinguishable from the traditional academic department, and the justification for their continued existence, *as an institute,* problematic. This is not to suggest that a selected institute should not, when appropriate, be converted to a department or school. Indeed, if an institute takes on the range of functions characteristic of a department, it may be incumbent on the university to change its status. But in so doing, its uniqueness as an institute will be lost.

V

Characteristics

Although it is important to understand certain general trends and qualities that characterize the origin, structure, and function of institutes, we also want to trace the evolution of what might be termed "inquiry networks" or families of institutes that have developed in response to specific national needs. Concern for environmental quality, for example, and the need to assure that the nation had a water supply of sufficient quantity and quality to meet the demands of an expanding population led to the establishment in the mid-sixties of a national network of water centers, a principle focus of our study. At about the same time, an inquiry network in the field of educational research was emerging, first in the form of research and development centers and later through a national network of "regional educational laboratories" sponsored, as were the water centers, by the federal government.

These two networks, one based on environmental concern and the other rooted in the dilemma of a widening gap between public expectations and the accomplishments of the schools, have in common a commitment to address a national need and sizable support from federal funds. They also illustrate important differences in the maturity and performance levels typical of institutes and centers in different disciplines.

Beyond Academic Departments

Water Centers

Abel Wolman, chairman of the Water Resources Study of the National Academy of Sciences-National Research Council, set forth a rationale for water centers, but he also suggested a line of reasoning applicable to many institutes and centers created during the post-World War II era. At the senate hearings (U.S. Senate, 1963) on the Water Resources Research Act, Wolman testified:

The most critical shortage in the field of water resources by far is the very real shortage of broadly trained people capable of planning and executing effective research programs. At present, we have no institutional structure in the United States to take care of multidisciplinary research in water. The whole hydrosciences field is now pathetically limited for the tasks involved. To strengthen it will require immediate provision of a program to enlist and train new people in a great many of the disciplines relating to water resources. The ultimate objective should be the development of a new structure and a new generation of well-rounded water scientists ready and able to approach the nation's multidisciplinary water-resources problems in a unified manner as "hydrosciences" (p. 10).

Interest in the development, use, and control of the nation's water resources paralleled our transformation from an agrarian to a highly industrialized and technologically oriented society. Water transportation was one of the first commercial activities regulated by the federal government. The abundance or scarcity of water for agricultural purposes was also an issue, but technologies to control or manipulate the environment were relatively unknown.

Immigration, westward expansion, and industrialization generated increased federal concern for water resources. Because of the general economic, social, recreational, and ecological significance of water, many government agencies over the years have

64

considered water resources their special province. In addition to the role of the Defense Department and its Corps of Engineers, the departments of Health, Education, and Welfare, Agriculture, Commerce, and the Interior were also heavily involved and concerned with these resources. As a result, many agencies assumed a propietary attitude toward the entire field of water resources.

Added to the parochialism, fragmentation, and competition on the national level was the parallel interest of the states and their opposition to more complete control by the national government in water resources planning. Use of the land-grant colleges and universities in each state to conduct research, it was thought, might allay state fears that their particular water-related environmental problems would receive scant attention. In addition, it was assumed that the universities might aid in disseminating knowledge and assistance to local agencies and officials concerned with water planning and management. The apparent success of land-grant institutions in agricultural research and public service provided a useful model.

During the Senate hearings on water resources, many experts testified in favor of using institutions of higher education for enlarging knowledge through research and for training scientists. Glenn T. Seaborg, subsequently chairman of the Atomic Energy Commission, stated that "science and the making of scientists go best together. . . . and when it can be managed, basic research should be done at, or at least in association with, universities" (U.S. Senate, 1963, p. 9).

Arthur W. Maass, professor of government at Harvard University and a leading authority on the politics of natural resources, also urged location of a national network of water centers at land-grant institutions: "Title I of this bill promotes continuing research on water resources in the land-grant colleges. This in my view is an admirable objective (because of)' . . . the success of this particular pattern of research in the field of agriculture; the need for water resources experts who can be trained in association with widely dispersed research programs in the land-grant colleges; geographical variations in water problems; and the desirability of strengthening state and local agencies concerned with water development by having research facilities available to them for advice and assistance" (p. 151).

As might be predicted, strong support for building the inquiry network of water centers within the land-grant system came from presidents, professors, and scientists from land-grant institutions as well as from representatives of professional societies and spokesmen for public and private conservation interest groups. Congressmen were already prone to choose the land-grant system, since the United States had no national university and perhaps the closest equivalent was the land-grant complex. By patterning the water center network on this model, each congressman also had the opportunity to serve his constituency and strengthen the prestige of his state institution.

The water resources legislation in 1964 called for the establishment of one center in each state and Puerto Rico, to be located at the land-grant college or university unless the state legislature designated some other institution. If there was more than one land-grant college in the state, and the state legislature took no action, decision-making authority rested with the governor (U.S. House of Representatives, 1964). No limitations were placed on the number of institutions that could share in the program, but to prevent unnecessary duplication, only one university could serve as the coordinating agency. Two or more states could cooperate in the designation of a single interstate or regional institute, in which case the sums assignable to all the cooperating states were paid to such an institute.

Prior to 1964, some land-grant universities were already engaged in water research to meet the special needs of their region. Water resources ranked as an important issue in many state legislatures (Francis, 1967). Several different institutional arrangements existed within the universities. Typically, a faculty member with a particular interest in these resources was given a modicum of funds, relatively free license, and encouragement to work on his own or, if he preferred, with others.

On at least two campuses, however, active water research

centers predated the federal legislation. Following the Texas drought of the 1950s, considerable pressure was exerted at the state level to develop a center for discussion of water problems within a university context. In 1952, a Water Research and Information Center was established at Texas A & M University. The Water Resources Center at the Los Angeles branch of the University of California developed after the state legislature during the 1956–1958 period requested a permanent organization to further the water-related research needs of the state.

Overall responsibility for administering the program of research and training was vested in the Office of Water Resources Research, United States Department of the Interior. The preamble of the Water Resources Act stated the purpose of the legislation: "In order to assist in assuring the nation at all times of a supply of water sufficient in quantity and quality to meet the requirement of its expanding population . . . to stimulate, sponsor, provide for, and supplement present programs for the conduct of research, investigations, experiments, and the training of scientists in the fields of water and of resources which affect water."

Continuing financial support was pledged to the newly established water centers under Title I of the Act. Although the Act called for the program to be subjected to congressional review in 1975, the size of the annual allotment available to each center increased over the period, in contrast to the decline in funds experienced in many other federally supported programs. In addition, the water centers profited by the requirement that the federal allotment could be used by the centers provided it was matched on a dollar-for-dollar basis by nonfederal funds, typically state-appropriated funds. The important net result was that each center had a modest financial base, was reasonably stable and almost invulnerable to vagaries of state funding and shifts of institutional, state, and federal priorities.

It is premature to judge how successful the water resources centers have been in achieving the goals for which they were created. Whether they will enable the nation to have at all times a "supply of water sufficient in quantity and quality" to meet the requirements of its expanding population is certainly not clear at this juncture and may never be fully discernible. One can, however, search for preliminary evidence.

First, it should be noted that the water resources inquiry network was completed essentially as initially designed. Fifty water centers were established, and all but three were in land-grant universities. Most operate at funding levels above the average typical for other university research institutes. Some water centers, for example, spend in excess of a million dollars a year. Congressional satisfaction is suggested by the gradual increase in the size of the annual federal allotment. Water centers have also enjoyed continuing support from the National Association of State Universities and Land Grant Colleges. Thus, while it is premature to judge the full impact of the water centers, the preliminary signs seem generally to be on the positive side.

Education Centers and Laboratories

Genuine federal concern and commitment to strengthen the nation's educational system began to take shape in the mid-1950s. Unlike the long-standing federal interest in water resources, significant federal involvement in the field of education began only as education came to be viewed as an instrument of national policy. Executive, legislative, and public support for increased federal investment in education was initially linked to international affairs—national defense to be more precise—culminating in the passage of the National Defense Education Act in the mid-1950s. As it became apparent that national policy concerns extended far beyond the initial preoccupation with national defense and into areas of economic development, racial equality, and the quality of life in the cities and rural areas, the nature and extent of federal involvement in education also broadened.

The bulk of federal support during the 1950s and 1960s went for direct improvement and reform of existing programs or the establishment of new programs in the nation's schools. Federal investment in educational research, however, also grew during this period, perhaps in belief that the educational establishment did not really know as much as it needed to know in order to spend the increased millions wisely. Many quarters expressed growing dissatisfaction with the effectiveness of the nation's educational system and a hope that increased investment in educational research would lead to greater effectiveness.

The Cooperative Research Act of 1954 marked the first significant effort by the federal government to support research and development in education. Patterned after most other federally sponsored research programs, the Cooperative Research Act channeled its funds through colleges and universities to individual professors and enabled them to carry on research programs largely of their own design and choosing. The technical excellence of the research proposal and the reputation of the principal investigator tended to outweigh any assumptions about national priorities for needed research and development.

Although the initial grants made under the Act were useful in strengthening the quality and quantity of educational research, criticism was also heard. Research programs in education, it was alleged, were too fragmented, with several different professors in different parts of the country working independently on related aspects of the same problem. Most research projects tended to be small-scale efforts that faculty members could carry out in connection with their professorial duties. Because of these limitations, research findings tended to be noncumulative and frequently inconclusive.

A second general class of complaints centered on the observation that the results of educational research and development did not appear to have a significant impact on changing practice in the classroom. Most projects took place within the university setting where the interests of the faculty and the reward system of the institution tended to favor research in preference to "development." Many research projects were never designed with a "product development" phase in mind, and so it was not surprising that results, while sometimes useful in theory buliding, frequently did not provide a sound base for developing improved products and procedures which would change significantly the quality of educational opportunity. Thus, while the Cooperative Research Act seemed to have stimulated educational research, it had not dramatically influenced the quality and quantity of educational development and did not seem to be reaching the ultimate goal of improved practice in the schools.

A third general criticism focused on the view that educational research was somehow not attracting a sufficiently wide range of talent or, more precisely, that the Cooperative Research program had been captured by the schools of education. Projects typically centered around the interests and capabilities of a single principal investigator, and as a consequence the research and development tended to be confined to his particular configuration of talents and perspectives. The curriculum experiments conducted during the mid-1950s by Educational Services, Inc., in fields such as physics and mathematics which drew together a broader range of talent including those from the disciplines as well as team members from the colleges of education and the public schools themselves seemed to suggest an attractive alternative organizational model for the conduct of educational research and development.

In response to these several concerns, the United States Office of Education initiated in 1963 a research and development center program. Conducted within the legislative framework of the Cooperative Research Act, the guidelines for the new program reflected the aspirations and expectations that led to its establishment:

> Research and development centers are designed to concentrate human and financial resources on a particular program area in education over an extended period of time in an attempt to make significant contributions toward an understanding of, and an improvement of educational practice in, the problem area. More specifically, the personnel of a center will:
>
> (1) Conduct basic and applied research studies, both of the laboratory and field type.

(2) *Conduct development activities designed to translate systematically research findings into educational materials or procedures, and field test the developed products.*

(3) *Demonstrate and disseminate information about the new programs or procedures which emerge from the research and development efforts. These activities may include demonstrations in a natural or operational setting, the preparation of films, tapes, displays, publications, and lectures, and the participation in symposia and conferences.*

(4) *Provide nationwide leadership in the chosen area* (*p. 27*).

The guidelines thus set the stage for the creation of the first federally sponsored inquiry network in the field of education. The strategy was three-pronged: to shift the highest priority from knowledge production alone to deliberate improvement of the relationship between the production and utilization of knowledge; to attract to educational research and development a greater range and diversity of multidisciplinary talent, especially talent residing outside of schools of education; and to create an instrumentality, in the form of research and development centers, in which investments could be made and through which an alternative to continued support of disconnected projects could be found (Mason and Boyan, 1968). "The cost of establishing and maintaining a center as an institution was seen, in large measure, as the price to be paid for initiating and managing continuous and cumulative programmatic efforts addressed to the solution of major problems" (p. 193).

During the next few years several research and development centers were established. Certain centers, such as the Wisconsin R & D Center for Cognitive Learning, enabled the earlier work of an education researcher to be broadened with an expanded emphasis on development and application, and to be placed on a programmatic rather than project-by-project support basis. Other centers, such as the Center for Research and Development in Higher Education located at the University of California (Berkeley), had been in existence prior to the initiation of the federal program and were able to shift their base from federal project support and foundation and institutional funds to the new system of programmatic support. Typically, centers were established in universities and involved individuals who had earlier demonstrated a high-level capacity for educational research and development; in this sense, the centers tended to build the inquiry network and to strengthen the critical mass of R & D talent.

The regional educational laboratories initiated in 1965 represented still a further evolution in government attempts to strike the appropriate institutional form for supporting educational research and development. The origin of this program is difficult to trace. In large part the laboratory program stemmed from the so-called Gardner Task Force on Education established in the summer of 1964 by President Johnson and also from essentially the same forces that led to the earlier research and development centers. Authority for the program was lodged unobtrusively in Title IV of the Elementary and Secondary Education Act of 1965. The Act as a whole was designed principally to provide compensatory education programs for educationally and economically disadvantaged students. Surprisingly, these laboratories were never mentioned explicitly in the Act. It was President Johnson in his message on education to Congress who made first public reference to regional educational laboratories and tied the laboratory program to Title IV. Title IV, in fact, was largely an extension of the earlier Cooperative Research Act of 1954, the legal base of the earlier research and development centers. Steven Bailey reported that during the five days of floor debate on the Elementary and Secondary Education Act, little attention was paid to Title IV by either house of Congress. Debate centered on the formula to be used to distribute the bulk of the money authorized under Title I of the Act (Bailey, 1970, p. 8).

The essential difference between the earlier research centers and the laboratories was the institutional or corporate structure of the proposed laboratories. The centers had been tied to universities; it soon became clear that those who administered the regional laboratory program had still another model in mind. Grants, in this instance, were to be given to nonuniversity-based scholars employed by quasi-nongovernmental organizations.

The traditional collegial system, rooted in the structure and mores of the academic department, was responsible in large part for the initiation of institutes and centers as an organization alternative. This system tended to value theoretical research rather than applied development and professorial autonomy rather than integrated teamwork. The creation of education centers was the first answer to this problem. The second and more radical step was to move educational research and development outside the corporate structure of the university. It was hoped that laboratories would be able to form a coalition extending beyond the universities to include state departments of education, local school systems, governing boards, business and industrial concerns, and social and cultural agencies having direct or indirect concern for improving education.

Following this model, a national network of twenty regional educational laboratories was established, theoretically blanketing the United States. From its inception, however, the program was beset by a series of trials and tribulations. The greatest single problem was the decision to bring the network into reality in one swift stroke by creating twenty laboratories rather than four or five. There was neither sufficient research and development talent to initiate an institution-building phase of this magnitude, nor the necessary management capability in the U.S. Office of Education to cope with the problems such a venture would inevitably generate.

As a result, national policy and guidelines for the regional laboratories tended to be formed on an ad hoc basis in response to specific problems. Laboratory directors and their boards of directors reponded to frequently changing policies and program directives from Washington while at the same time conducting a frantic search for talented staff that simply was not available in the quantity and quality implied by the decision to move quickly to a level of twenty laboratories.

A second major setback for the laboratory progarm was its level of funding. The initial vision for the laboratory program was *big.* Each laboratory was to receive five to ten million dollars a year by the end of the first five years of operation. Some of the initial laboratory prospectuses projected ultimate funding levels of twenty million dollars or more annually. But as the costs of Vietnam mounted and inflation accelerated, the pressure grew to cut federal spending. Most vulnerable were the "controllable" expenditures for research, especially those for programs of recent vintage and those lacking strong and vocal constitutencies. The laboratory program qualified on every count. Although dedicated efforts by HEW staff prevented many threatened cutbacks, the funding base never grew, and uncertainty was the norm. The program became overextended, with insufficient resources to nourish adequately the existing network. Partly because of the funding crisis and partly because of generally recognized weak programs and institutions, the number of laboratories was cut essentially in half as federal support for several laboratories was discontinued.

A third broad category of problems stemmed from their corporate structure. The laboratories were neither fish nor fowl. They were not government agencies, for they had their own corporate and governing structures. Neither were they in any sense independent of the Office of Education that supplied 100 per cent of the financial support for most labs. The board of directors generally represented the various segments of the educational community to which each laboratory related. Increasingly, however, the real "governance" came from Washington as Office of Education personnel realized that they, not the laboratory boards, would ultimately be held accountable by the legislative and executive branches of government.

The broader question of whether the establishment of regional laboratories outside the corporate structure of universities achieved the desired ends is still far from answered. The action, in most instances, did remove the laboratories from the domination of the research orientation and the traditions of professorial autonomy characteristically associated with universities. Whether the weakening of university ties was accompanied by a significant strengthening of bonds with other constituencies that could not

74

have been accomplished in the university setting is less clear. It is certainly not at all evident that the hoped-for breadth and quality of laboratory staffing was realized. It is quite possible that a stronger staff could have been built within the university corporate structure. Irrespective of these concerns, however, the ultimate test for the laboratories—their impact on improved educational practices in the nation's schools—remains unanswered.

Thus, the research and development centers and the network of regional educational laboratories reflect alternative answers to a single problem: what organizational structure is most conducive to the conduct of programmatic educational research and development and most efficient in ensuring the appropriate application of findings and products to the educational enterprise? Both provide alternatives to the more conventional option of the lone professor and his department. Time may be instructive to the federal government as it seeks wiser answers to the question. In the case of universities, the question is one of mission: Is it the role of the university to attempt to bring about constructive change in education, or in agriculture, or in other fields of social concern, and if so, how can the university organize itself to go about the task more effectively?

Social Science–Humanities Institutes

Tracing the growth and development of the wide variety of institutes in the social sciences and humanities is a formidable task. Unlike the water centers and the centers and laboratories in education, these institutes have no single history or a common date of origin. One can find few references in the *Congressional Record* that articulate the goals, and there are no administrative guidelines to standardize procedures.

Institutes in the social sciences and humanities are unequal partners, the former far outnumbering the latter. If longevity were a crucial variable, however, institutes in the humanities would have the advantage. Both the medieval and the modern university had, at their core, scholarship in the liberal arts and humanistic studies.

Despite its antiquity, however, research in the humanities has often been considered an expendable luxury in a complex technological society, and this attitude is reflected in the paucity of institutes engaged in humanistic scholarship and research. Equally important is the possibility that humanistic research may not require the highly organized setting provided by the institute structure. The number of social science institutes has increased sharply in recent years, perhaps because of faith or belief in the ability of the social sciences to contribute to the solution of societal problems, but also reflecting the growing complexity and scale of research programs in these fields.

Several historical considerations have had a significant impact on the development of social science institutes. Betz and Kruytbosch (1970) traced the development of the research function at the University of California (Berkeley)' and cited the long-standing state support provided for organized research units that performed services for the state. A close look at social science and humanities institutes reveals that the majority have a strong public service orientation.

Institutes with a political science base were frequently designed to help upgrade the level of personnel in the public sector, offer consultative services to state and local governmental officials, and through publications and short courses to keep public officials abreast of new techniques. It is not uncommon for such units also to offer professional graduate degree programs in areas such as public administration. In the course of their work many of these institutes have developed political contacts at the state level that have been useful to their continuity. Some have even received special line-item appropriations from the state in the university's budget.

Bureaus of business and economic research, perhaps under the aegis of the department of economics or the school of business administration, are further examples of public service-oriented institutes in the social sciences. The service typically provided to the state's industrial leaders is illustrated by the following statement of mission: "Business and economic data can be secured by original investigations and/or compilations from other sources. The Bureau can determine, for example, a community's trading area and the socioeconomic characteristics of the area's inhabitants. The number of potential customers, where and why they last bought selected items and services, and their shopping habits and opinions on shopping conditions can be ascertained by survey."

A third class of social science institutes is illustrated by the Survey Research Center at the University of Michigan. The center began as a U.S. Department of Agriculture service that was subsequently moved to the university by its principal organizers. From its inception, the center has been able to undertake large-scale research projects because of its staff of well-trained and highly specialized technicians and professionals. In addition to devising measurement techniques, the center has conducted several studies related to organizational, economic, and political behavior. The Survey Research Center and the National Opinion Research Center of the University of Chicago are only two of the well-known university-based research institutes of this genre and to a limited extent represent archetypes that other centers have tried to emulate.

The realization that the social sciences could be useful in solving the nation's problems gained ascendancy during the early New Deal period, a period during which the nation was plagued by a number of persistent social and economic problems. President Roosevelt relied heavily on the counsel of social scientists for policy directives and legislative proposals, including both the initial social security legislation and the first Federal Wage and Hour Law. John Maynard Keynes' theory that prosperity could be restored by increased government spending was looked upon with suspicion by his British compatriots but formed the basis of Roosevelt's recovery program. Although there are still debates over whether the application of Keynesian principles was and is the best solution for economic crises, the important fact is that Keynes' work signaled a growing acceptance of economics and other social sciences as useful in formating social policy.

Research in the social sciences also became highly technical during this period. The acceptance of the problem-solving capability of the social sciences came slowly, and in the search for

77

acceptance, social scientists frequently borrowed the terminology and methodology of the physical and life sciences. Perhaps the "turning inward" during the McCarthy era also contributed to the new methods, since research of an empirical or quantitative nature and the use of mathematical tools and models were viewed as somewhat less controversial.

The decade of the sixties ushered the social scientists back into the inner circles and the public eye. Racial tension and the decline of the cities were persistent and only too obvious national crises. Voter registration drives, lunch-counter sit-ins, and enforced desegregation of school districts, particularly in the South, pitted black against white. The middle class was fleeing to the suburbs at an accelerated rate, leaving the cities without an adequate tax base to handle the rising crime rate or additional welfare burden caused by the urban poor. Balance of payments problems, a war in Indochina, and environmental pollution joined the list of national concerns, and the expectation that a solution for these problems might somehow be found in the social sciences also grew. Growth in the number of social science institutes and centers was an integral part of this evolution.

Physical and Life Science Institutes

Very early in the history of American colleges and universities there was a modest amount of federal investment in the sciences, especially those that emphasized the applied aspects of their research. Following the passage of the Hatch Act of 1887, land-grant universities received funds for operating agricultural experiment stations. Although the principal focus was on agricultural problems, the pioneer work carried out by the experiment stations had far greater scientific impact. Many prominent geneticists and biochemists received their initial training in this setting. Engineering experiment stations were also established, along with herbariums, museums, and laboratories that served as teaching aids. Perhaps the greatest contribution of these early efforts was the legitimization of research as an appropriate function in the American university.

It was American involvement in World War II, however, that catapulted the sciences into national prominence and boosted their stocks considerably. From the beginning of the industrial revolution, western society acknowledged its dependence on science and the by-products of that technology. The success of the Manhattan Project elevated the status of scientific research. The number of institutes and centers in the sciences grew rapidly. Among the land-grant institutions, approximately two-thirds of all institutes and centers are research arms of the basic and applied sciences (Ikenberry, 1970).

As was suggested earlier, the emergence of institutes forged a new pattern of interpersonal relations among college faculty members. It was not a coincidence that prominent scientists from many universities could collaborate with each other, unravel the secrets of the atom, and produce the most deadly weapon the world had ever known. The socialization process by which graduate students in the sciences became full-fledged members of a discipline nurtured this collaborative capacity. As a result, physical or life scientists are likely to be "team players." Their doctoral research is often part of a larger, grand design. Laboratories, cyclotrons, and other sophisticated equipment are essential to support their work, and thus they are frequently dependent on the assistance of other scientists. Joint or multiple authorship of research papers is common and even the most prestigious awards in science, such as Nobel prizes, are often shared by eminent scholars working in collaboration with each other. In short, the sciences set the model, of means as well as ends, that led to the growth of organized research in the university and to the consequent proliferation of research institutes and centers.

Although scientific research was firmly ensconced in the university setting in the decade after 1945, it was the nation's major space effort, related to the advent of Sputnik, that gave a major boost to national investment in science. As a result of the Soviet feat, certain disciplines, such as astronomy and mathematics, received proportionately larger investments. There were few astronomical observatories in operation at land-grant universities prior to Sputnik, but the growth pattern is noteworthy. The distribution tended to be bimodal: Most of the observatories were established either before 1940 or after Sputnik in 1957. Fear of Russian scientific supremacy activated renewed interest in the entire educational system, and federally funded, university-instigated "think tanks" brought about major revisions in the public school science and mathematics curricula. The renewed interest in science also had a ripple effect, stimulating research across the board in the social sciences, humanities, and education as well as in the physical and life sciences. It generated a virtual tidal wave of public concern and financial support that continued into the late 1960s. And then, characteristically, a shift of national priorities away from defense and space-oriented research in the sciences resulted in weakened financial support for nearly all programs.

Summary and Conclusions

Some of the unique features of institutes and centers make comparison difficult. While some centers were encouraged, promoted, or even designed by government agencies, others emerged with little or no government influence. In some instances, centers at one university have entered into formal, continuous alliances with similarly constituted units at other universities. But the presence or absence of a formal alliance does not deny the existence of the informal inquiry network that tends to develop among centers. The directors and the center staffs, therefore, must respond not only to their own desires and to the direction of the university administration, they must be aware of the activities in several other academic units similar to their own. For some of the directors, the organization chart and communication channels are unavoidably complex and unbelievably tortuous.

Despite the apparent homogeneity within a single class of institutes, there is wide divergence. Among water centers, for example, each has "seed money" from federal sources. But some water centers are barely able to match federal funds with additional monies while others have contracts in excess of half a million dollars. Some water centers do not employ a full-time director while others have a payroll of fifty or more people. A few of the institutes are reasonably well-located and accessible to the main campus, and a few are relegated to obscure quarters.

Physical and life science institutes, as a group, are the best supported, internally and externally, and display the accouterments befitting their status: well-equipped laboratories, office space, large full-time professional staffs, graduate students, and postdoctoral fellows. In their wooing of research contracts, they operate from a position of strength, having already amassed sizable inventories of equipment and a considerable number of highly trained specialists. For every university dollar invested in their operation, they generate four additional dollars from external sources. But such larger organizations may have the most difficult adjustment in a period of changing priorities.

Position within the university's organizational structures apparently offers no meaningful clues about the quality or range of operations of institutes. It is true that the social science-humanities institutes are somewhat more likely than are the other two types to be organized within departments; the least viable organizations tended to cluster at that level. Many institutes existed at a minimum level, with considerable dependence on the academic department. Some institutes appeared to be "wholly owned" subsidiaries of the sponsoring departments, and both funding and staffing were heavily influenced by departmentally assigned priorities and the prevailing disciplinary values. As one respondent stated, "The establishment of a fully funded research center *in* an academic department adds overall strength to the research and service capacity of the department without undermining the discipline."

Universities, like other institutions in American society, tend to mirror the prevailing fads and fashions of the times. Many institutes have chalked up an enviable record and a list of notable achievements. With good reason, these institutes approach the

81

future with optimism. For many others, however, there is a rough road ahead. Although their record of achievement may have been no more spotted than that of many an academic department, institutes remain more vulnerable, and many will be and should be phased out in the years ahead. To phase out or to strengthen a weak institute is not to deny the contribution to university functioning of this organizational form. We do suggest, however, that much is still to be learned about building and maintaining strong and well functioning academic organizations.

VI

Control

Although the organizational structure of the university has changed over the last two decades with the introduction of institutes and centers, the locus of power in academe and the ability to control rewards and sanctions remains much the same. The academic departments have, if anything, strengthened their power base. Departments continue to exert the principal force in the operational definition of goals and purposes of the university; they largely control faculty reward mechanisms; and they are, through both formal and informal mechanisms, the primary focus of institutional progress and academic achievement.

Institutes and centers tend to be excluded from these circles. Their directors and professional staff members, by virtue of institutional policy, have very limited powers in decision areas such as rank, tenure, salary, and promotions. It is not surprising, therefore, that such personnel policies and practices generate conflict from time to time between institute directors and department chairmen and between professional staff members employed in institutes and departmental faculty members. The unanswered question, of course, is whether such conflict contributes to the effectiveness of institutes and to the university as a whole or whether it is merely disruptive.

Departmental Power

Most universities apparently have few formal, written policies that define power relationships between institutes and departments. In response to the question "Does the university have a written policy regarding the employment of professional personnel in organized research units?" nearly two-thirds of the forty-six university administrators indicated that the institution had no such policy. With or without a formal written policy, however, there was substantial agreement on key policy questions such as the award of tenure, eligibility for membership in the senate, award of professorial rank, and promotion of professional staff members employed in institutes. In each case, control tended to rest with the academic department.

Several policy statements emphasized that institutes and centers are established "to aid the research and enhance the teaching of participating members of the faculty." Public service, it was added, may be a coordinate objective (Utah State University, 1968). A report of the University of California (Berkeley) senate (Academic Plan Steering Committee, 1968) suggested a similar orientation when it observed: "A major issue in this regard is the appropriate level of nonsenate professional staffing. Evidently the senate's Academic Plan Steering Committee regards the present high ratio of nonsenate professional staff to senate participants as a cause for concern."

Some observers understand the principal function of institutes to be the enhancement of career opportunities and professional activities of senior faculty members and the prestige of their departments. Within such a framework, the control of institutes by academic departments is seen as not only appropriate but perhaps essential. Others, such as Steinhart and Cherniack (1969), believe that the weak power position of institutes and centers results in "ineffectiveness."

University policies tend to allow considerable freedom and autonomy to institutes and centers in the appointment of professional personnel as long as professorial rank is not involved. In all but two universities, institute appointments not involving professorial rank required no formal approval by any departmental or senate committee. Most of the universities (83 per cent) reported that salary increases recommended for professional personnel in institutes did not have to be reviewed by any academic department or senate committee as long as the staff member did not hold a joint appointment in an academic department. Fringe benefits, such as insurance plans and retirement programs, were reported to be essentially the same for those holding only research appointments and for department staff holding professorial rank.

The rights and privileges, as well as the academic values, implied by professorial rank, however, cause most professional staff members to seek this rank as part of the initial terms of appointment. In nearly two-thirds of the universities surveyed, professional staff members could not hold professorial rank, such as professor or associate professor, solely on the basis of their appointment in an institute or center. Such titles could be awarded only by academic departments. Thus, the autonomy of institutes is restricted significantly by the need to gain departmental concurrence with most professional-level appointments.

The harsh truth in most universities, especially the higher prestige, graduate, and research-oriented institutions, is that in order to be *of* the university and not just *at* it, one must be a member of *the* faculty. And faculty status, in most such universities, is available only through departmental affiliation. The University of Wisconsin policy statement (1970, p. 2) is instructive: "Tenure academic staff positions include professors and associate professors *who have been appointed in departments.* . . . they also include assistant professors and instructors who have been granted tenure" (emphasis added). With reference to appointments as scientists or fellows in research institutes and centers, the policy notes: "These academic staff positions include a variety of academic *roles performed in support of* the university's mission. While none carries with it tenure, probationary, or University Faculty status implications, appointees are not precluded from consideration from latter designation (p. 3)'.

Beyond Academic Departments

More than three-quarters of the university administrators estimated that most professional staff members in institutes on their campus also held appointments in an academic department. Interestingly, the practice of joint appointments tended to be somewhat more prevalent in universities with fewer institutes and with graduate programs of somewhat lower status in terms of the Cartter report. Such is not to suggest that departmental control is any weaker in the more research-oriented, higher status institutions but, on the contrary, that access to full faculty membership and privileges in the academic community is even more restricted in such institutions. The frustrations of "unequal peers" in a high-status, research-oriented university were revealed by Kruytbosch and Messinger (1968). In their analysis of "The Situation of Researchers at Berkeley," they reported several important differences in university policy and practice between departmental faculty members and researchers with only institute or center appointments. The researcher, for example, could not obtain membership in the senate or in other important university policy-making bodies; he was not eligible for an award of tenure or for paid leaves of absence. He could not participate, as could his colleagues in academic departments, in the institutional appointments and promotions process and at Berkeley apparently did not even enjoy the same parking and library privileges. The size of the research program at Berkeley, combined with the formal institutional policy and informal faculty traditions, apparently created two classes of professional employees, one of which was disenfranchised and worked essentially on the fringe of the university community.

The clash between the "two worlds" of institutes and departments is not severe in most universities. Yet administrators' reports of institutional policy tend to confirm departmental control. Among the universities which provided access to senate membership for professional staff members employed solely in an institute (nearly three-quarters), such access was more likely to be available in those universities with smaller doctoral programs and with graduate programs of lower standing as appraised by the Cartter report. In short, the data suggest that the strength of the departments and disciplines is inversely related to the power and autonomy of institutes.

For staff members holding joint appointments in academic departments and institutes, the policy of about half the universities allowed recommendations for promotion to originate in the institute as well as in the department. In the remaining half, initiation of promotion recommendations was limited to the academic department. In either case, nearly all universities required the concurrence of the academic department. And, again, the heavier the institution's involvement in sponsored research, the more likely the requirement of departmental approval.

Joint appointment in an academic department is not necessarily a mere courtesy gesture. In a large number of responding universities (44 per cent), joint appointment of a staff member by a center and a department required a salary payment from the budgets of both units. Salary can also become an issue in the award of annual merit increases. The policy of most universities (78 per cent) required that salary increases recommended for institute staff members holding joint appointments be approved by the academic departments.

The extent of departmental control is also illustrated by the fact that more than one-third of the universities reported that a professional staff member who did not hold professorial rank could not serve as principal investigator for an institute project. Thus, although institutes might be allowed to appoint professional personnel without departmental approval, they would not be authorized to assign them principal-investigator status without that approval. Review of the few available written policy statements suggested that it was either generally expected or, in fact, required that the director of an institute or center be "concurrently a regular tenure member of the faculty" (University of California, 1963, p. 3).

Apart from the control of standard perquisites of salary, tenure, rank, and promotion, departments exercise other controls when they choose to use them, including access to teaching opportunities and a voice in curriculum decisions. The Utah State

University policy statement (1968, p. 1), reflecting standard practice, specifies that no organized research unit shall offer regular academic curricula or confer degrees, but that it may provide research training to students employed in its research program. For those professional staff members who seek career opportunities and satisfactions other than research, as most do, departmental relationships are extremely important.

It is apparent that there are rather sharp restrictions on institute autonomy with respect to academic personnel policies in most universities. An additional limitation is that institutes are among the few organizational units that are not expected, and indeed may not be allowed, to develop a permanent professional staff. In seventy per cent of the universities, formal or informal policy declared that organized research units generally should not develop full-time permanent professional staffs but should draw on rotating and part-time joint faculty appointments from academic departments.

The policy statement of the State University of New York is quite clear on this matter: "As a general rule, units as established under these policies shall not have a permanent or quasi-permanent staff except for the necessary administrative assistants and technical and clerical staff. Exceptions are permissible for units with heavy public service responsibilities giving rise to need for permanent positions. This rule shall not preclude the continuing employment of regular faculty members on a split appointment basis or nonfaculty research appointments for the duration of specific research projects" (Porter, 1965, p. 4). Faculty members concerned about career stability may find the institute too unpredictable and seek a more permanent home in an academic department. One might also suspect that some faculty members associated jointly with institutes and departments might be inclined to give first priority to the demands of the department, assuming this relationship to be the more lasting of the two.

Academic departments also exercise control through their power, sometimes formal and sometimes informal, to evaluate the performance of institutes. Just as institute appointments are expected to be temporary, some institutes are expected to have a finite life. Interviews with university administrators revealed that although few centers had really been dissolved, they tended nonetheless to be regarded as temporary in mission, if not in structure. Some university policies call for periodic review of the goals and accomplishments of institutes. The University of California policy statement (1963), for example, requires that "at five-year intervals each unit shall be examined by a special review committee appointed by the appropriate Chief Campus Officer or by the President. The examining committee shall submit a report appraising need for the continuation of the unit. The purposes for which the unit was initially funded and the emergence of further or changed aims shall be reviewed in the report. Such reports shall be reviewed by the Academic Senate Committee on Educational Policy" (p. 3).

To the extent that such policy statements are actually taken seriously, academic departments can be in a position to pass judgment on the performance of institutes. If the university senate figures prominently in such a review, as is the case at Berkeley, it is the tenured faculty with professorial rank in academic departments who will be called upon to make the judgments. Informal appraisals of a given institute or center can be transmitted through the institutional hierarchy by deans and department chairmen. The policy statement of the State University of New York declares that "the normal unit for instruction and research is the department" (Porter, 1965, p. 1). Certainly this is the case in most if not all universities. It follows that the normal—the academic department—will usually evaluate the deviant—the institute or center—and not the other way around.

Advisory Committees

Power and authority tend to be diffused in the complex university, but the diffusion is especially acute with respect to institutes. Organizational tension between institutes and their external environment is considerable at times. The pressures come from all sides: Departments can exercise controls over appointments, promotions, and salary adjustments for faculty members; deans may wish to exercise greater control over the expenditure of institute resources for purposes that may or may not be in accord with the principal mandate of the institute; temporary professional staff members of the institute may be unresponsive to institute needs because of competing priorities and rewards in their academic departments.

External pressures are also common. The funding agency, for example, may press for immediate, highly practical results at the expense of longer term and more fundamental approaches to problem-solving preferred by the institute; pressures to audit, censor, or classify research publications are sometimes faced; and a wide range of pluralistic and sometimes conflicting publics demand to be served.

Whatever the origin of pressures and tensions, institutes must identify and manage the conflict, maintain at least minimally satisfactory working relationships within the university and with its constitutents and, over time, gain the confidence and the support of these disparate groups sufficiently to sustain the life and productivity of the institute. Advisory committees are apparently useful mechanisms toward such ends.

Several elements may instigate establishment of these committees. Policies of some universities require or strongly encourage them. Research sponsors may make clear their desire for the formation of a committee, as did the Office of Water Resources Research. Or center directors may wish to form an advisory committee for their own purposes. Whatever the motive, some three-quarters of the 125 institutes and centers in the study have such a committee. Nearly all the water centers, 94 per cent, had one. Among social science institutes, the least likely of the three groups to have one, a majority reported having a committee.

The composition of the committees varied widely. In some cases membership came almost entirely from the local campus, while in other instances members were drawn in full from outside the university. The most common configuration was composed principally of deans, department chairmen, and other influential individuals on the local campus. Although institutes in the social sciences were somewhat less likely to have an advisory committee, those that did tended to draw the entire membership from the local campus or from a combination of local and external sources. The roles and positions represented by committee members are suggested by this partial listing: heads of departments related to research efforts; deans of engineering, agriculture, mines, and forestry; graduate school and college deans or their representative; four state officials, three federal officials, four industrialists; professional scientists in the petroleum industry; ten labor representatives and twelve faculty members. Committees tended to draw their membership from potential adversaries, perhaps in the hope of gaining better cooperation and resolving differences, or from useful allies who would be potential defenders of the institute in a time of crisis, or both.

The data suggest that the role of advisory committees can be better understood from a political perspective—identification, management, and resolution of conflict—than from a scientific or technical perspective, although some committees probably play both roles. In appraising its contributions, few institute directors reported or implied that the committee gave significant scientific or technical advice important to the conduct of the institute's research. The more typical comments were as follows:

"It serves as an administrative double-check."

"In general, it acts to protect the interests of committee members."

"Initially, it was very beneficial in establishing internal protocol."

"It enhances acceptance and support of our center."

"It gives sanction for changes which we suggest."

"Members are links to agencies they represent."

"It aids in dissemination of information to interested parties."

Among the ninety-four institutes and centers that used an advisory committee, 42 per cent of the directors described the committee's role in terms of conflict identification and management, building interpersonal and interorganizational relationships, and strengthening public relations. An additional 33 per cent reported that the committee played a kind of low-keyed, general advisory role. In the remaining 25, per cent of the cases, the directors reported candidly that the committee was, in fact, nonfunctional.

There was an almost total failure to attribute any significant governance or decision-making role to advisory committees. When asked to evaluate the impact of the committee on institute policy and programs, a majority of the directors rated the influence as modest or almost nonexistent. There were some apparent differences among institutes on this point, however. Water center directors, for example, were more likely than other directors to attribute a significant role to the advisory committee: 14 per cent rated advisory committee influence as strong, while an additional 44 per cent rated it as fairly strong. Directors in the social and physical sciences rated the committee as having a modest or nonexistent impact.

We suspected that advisory committees might function as protective devices in the early formative stages of institute development, but then gradually decline in relative importance. Responses from directors did not fully support this proposition. Although several did report a reduction in committee activity or the actual discontinuation of a committee after a period of time, the general pattern suggested that committee influence continued and, in several instances, increased in strength following the institute's initial period of operation.

Program Control

We attempted to assess the relative influence of various forces, including advisory committees, on the research programs of institutes. How important, for example, were vice-presidents for research and university senates in influencing the direction of institute programs? To what extent did funding agencies call the tune? What was the role of professional staff members in shaping program objectives?

Control

Institute directors were asked to rank several forces in terms of their relative influence on their programs. Directors of water centers, social science centers, and physical and life science institutes all agreed that the most potent influence in shaping the program was the director himself. The great majority of directors ranked their influence at the top or next to the top. Such rankings may be regarded by some as possible overestimates of one's own importance, but as Rossi (1964) has observed, "Characteristically, institutes and centers have 'directors' while departments have 'chairmen,' expressing in the titles of their chief administrative officers the greater authority of the one as compared with the other" (p. 1150). Rossi went on to point out that, in his view, institutes and centers functioned best when the director provided strong intellectual and administrative leadership. Effective leadership may be even more important in institutes than in departments because of the need of institutes to preserve their task or problem orientation and coordinate the work of teams of individuals.

Following general agreement that directors exerted the greatest influence on center program and policy, the rankings of other forces tended to be more dispersed. Water center directors, for example, tended to rank the advisory committee as the next most important influence in shaping their programs. Ten per cent of these directors ranked the advisory committee as the single most important influence and an additional 32 per cent ranked it second only to the director. Social and physical-life science institute directors were much less likely to attribute this degree of effect to the committee and tended to rank it toward the bottom of the list.

The second most influential force in program determination reported by social and physical-life science directors was the professional staff. More than half the directors in each group ranked professional staff first or second in terms of relative influence. Water center directors, by contrast, ascribed much less impact to staff: Only 28 per cent ranked professional staff members first or second in relative importance. The heavy reliance on part-time appointments in water centers and the close identification of staff members with their academic departments may be related to the apparently restricted program influence of professional staff in these centers.

Water centers also deemphasized vice-presidents for research. Most institute directors said research vice-presidents had only a moderate effect on programs, but water center directors tended to give them an even lower ranking than did the others. Funding agencies were also ranked in the middle levels, although water center directors appeared to accord a bit more importance to their influence than did directors in the other categories. Directors were in near unanimous agreement that university senates or other faculty groups did not exert a powerful influence on their research programs. Senates were ranked last or next to last in relative influence by more than 90 per cent of all directors.

Summary and Conclusions

The autonomy of institutes and centers is constrained by a variety of forces. Universities place certain general restrictions on the range of functions they can perform. Offering courses, setting up curricula, and granting degrees, for example, are not legitimate activities in most units. Use of the project proposal as a principal funding device further restricts legitimate functions and requires staff members to allocate their time and energies in general accord with formal contract agreements.

Departments exercise control over appointment of professional staff and over decisions concerning rank, promotion, tenure, and salary adjustments. In certain extreme instances, they make such decisions unilaterally without consulting the institute director. Consequently, many institute staff members have strong ties and loyalties to their academic departments and see their relationships with the institute as temporary.

Advisory committees restrict autonomy still further. Potential academic competitors of institutes, such as department chairmen or deans, may be placed on advisory committees as a means of resolving and managing conflict. The advisory committee may be useful as a moderating force and in resolving conflict and tensions, but it can also contribute to further conflict and a reduction of institute autonomy.

The funding agency, the institute director, and the institute staff all compete for power and influence. The grantor has every right to expect his wishes to be served. The institute director carries a major share of the burden of institute survival and naturally feels he should call the shots. And the professional integrity and academic freedom of professional staff urge that decisions come from the bottom up rather than top down. No wonder the question "who's in charge?" arises.

The interesting question is whether such conditions and constraints contribute to the strength of institutes or whether they restrict and retard effectiveness. Directors were asked to report the two or three most vexing problems, frustrations, or difficulties they encountered in their work. Their responses suggest that the problems they experience are similar to those faced by other university administrators. One director commented, for example, that his most vexing problems were a "lack of recognition, lack of space, lack of top-notch personnel, and lack of funds." Resource shortages, common in any organization, were frequently mentioned as problems by the directors.

The impact of constraints on autonomy was also evident in their replies. Most prominent were problems stemming from relationships with academic departments. They mentioned antagonistic attitudes of discipline-focused faculty members and administrators who maintained an almost exclusive commitment to their departments rather than to the work of the institute. Other difficulties were less pervasive, such as the problem of getting reports in on time from departmental faculty members. Numerous comments revealed that departmental control of important rewards and sanctions incited problems over split appointments, divided time, and loyalties.

The operational autonomy of institute directors seems unduly restricted in some universities, especially in institutions whose departments exercise unusually powerful controls. An increase in autonomy and liberation from excessive departmental control might well strengthen institute effectiveness. The director, like any other

95

responsible middle-level academic administrator, dean, or department chairman, must be able to exercise relatively unobstructed control over expenditures if he is to be held accountable by the university and by the funding agency for the use of resources. Subversion of institute resources for separate departmental purposes, a price for peace mentioned by a few directors, appears intolerable.

Directors need strengthened mechanisms to deal more effectively with irresponsible and inadequate performance by faculty members. Several directors had difficulty in securing completed research reports and in getting faculty members appointed on a temporary basis to fulfill their responsibilities. One water center director reported no problems at all along these lines: He merely withheld a portion of each month's salary for the duration of the project, payable on receipt of the final research report! Such drastic action is neither possible nor desirable in most institutions, but other measures are needed to increase the responsiveness of staff members to the institute's priorities.

VII

Institutes and the University

The fundamental issue of this study is the place of institutes in the university. Are they useful additions to the university's organizational configuration, or do they only verify the confused purposes, the fragmentation of structure, and the dissipation of resources some claim are part of the problem? These questions are not easily answered, for they relate to basic assumptions about the fundamental goals of the university.

Few components of the university have been criticized as sharply or frequently by students, faculty, and administrators as have institutes and centers. They allege that institutes undermine the teaching function and distract faculty from a dispassionate pursuit of truth. Substituted is a kind of academic capitalism, an orientation toward profit rather than education. The results are distorted academic reward structures and confused university purposes. Another frequent criticism is that institutes, at the very least, have complicated an already impossible organizational structure. These criticisms must be faced, but to do so we must first tackle those assumptions about the nature of the university.

97

Beyond Academic Departments

Purposes of the University

Essays on the objective of the university are legion, and yet none is definitive. Clark Kerr and others hold that the university has no single purpose but rather multiple purposes held together by a single corporate structure. The distinction between university and multiversity reflects the shift from the essential unity in the pre–World War II university to the present state of multipurposes, some of which may be in apparent conflict and contradiction. The classical view is that the university has no purposes, at least none as defined in utilitarian terms. The pursuit of truth is synonymous with purpose and the means are ends in themselves. The primary function of the corporate body, therefore, is to provide a setting for scholarly activity.

The debate is not new. Francis Bacon several centuries ago argued against an adoration of the mind. Bacon postulated that knowledge should be used for the benefit of man, that it gained meaning as it was put to use. Cardinal Newman, in his *Idea of a University* (1960), set forth the contrary view: that knowledge is capable of being its own end and needs no utilitarian defense. The clash between these two apparently conflicting philosophies is at the root of the differing views about the place of institutes. Is the university a means toward more important social goals, or are the pursuit of truth and maintenance of the academic community necessary and sufficient ends?

Those who want the university to be without utilitarian purpose ask for an improbable luxury. Knowledge is the fuel central to a scientific, technological, and socially complex society; it is the nourishment society must have to function and prosper. The rapid escalation of the power of the university results from its role in the knowledge industry as a principal producer and distributor. From this point of view, one could argue persuasively that the raison d'être of the contemporary university is not knowledge for its own sake but knowledge for society's sake.

Recognition of the social utility of universities does not require them to be totally subservient to day by day variance in

social whim or preference. Hard-won traditions of academic freedom were designed, in large part, to protect not only scholars but
their institutions from those repressive forces in all ages that would
bend the truth to conform to their own beliefs and purposes. What
must be argued and reargued within the academy, for it is easily
forgotten, is that a university must not be conceived principally
as an instrument of present-day society and its value judged solely
in terms of its immediate and obvious usefulness. Social utility, in
other words, must be assessed with the perspective of time and with
a broad view of institutional purposes.

While recognizing the difficulty of making short-term judgments of social utility, the requirement that the university relate
itself to the needs of society is in no way relieved. Colleges and
universities are among the social institutions most vulnerable to the
hazards of goal displacement. Means can be substituted for ends,
and the immediate gratification of professional needs may precede
social requirements. Those who call for increased accountability—
legislatures, governmental agencies, students, the courts, governing
boards, foundations, the press, and the general public—no doubt
believe that the relationship between what the university does and
what society needs is not as direct and as strong as it should be.
The proposition "knowledge for society's sake" asks the university
to reexamine the requirements of the world and the nature of its
efforts to meet them. Those who support institutes tend to view
them as an important instrument in strengthening this bond between
university programs and societal needs.

Those within universities, however, tend to see the matter
differently. Faculty members, for example, usually view the university in nonutilitarian terms. In a survey of university goals,
Gross and Grambsch (1968) were able to identify seven on which
there was general agreement within the academic community. The
highest purpose of the university according to faculty members,
was to protect their right to academic freedom. Other goals, ranked
in order of importance, included the need to maintain the prestige
of the university and top quality in those programs felt to be especially important; ensure the confidence and support of those who

contribute to finances and other material resource needs; keep up to date and responsive; train students in methods of scholarship, scientific research, and/or creative endeavor; and carry on pure research. This cluster of objectives regarded by faculty members to be most important could hardly be faulted as overly utilitarian. Interestingly, the goal accorded least significance in a list of forty-seven was to make a good consumer of the student—a person who is elevated culturally, has good taste, and can make good consumer choices.

Added to this nonutilitarian characterization is the claim that colleges and universities are different from organizations in the business and industrial sector. The nature of the difference and its implications, however, are not well understood either by those within the academic community or by society at large. The major distinction lies in the inability of higher education institutions to clearly define their goals and purposes and to build their organizational structure in accord with them. The Gross and Grambsch study indicates this lack of clarity: Most of the goals ranked highest in importance tend to be support goals, not functional ones. Maintenance of the academic community and the academic life style has become synonymous, in the minds of many, with the ultimate purposes of the university.

One need look no further than college catalogs to document the difficulty experienced by academic organizations in defining their objectives. Statements of institutional purpose frequently communicate little of the significant educational goals of the institution. The translation is accomplished primarily through the curriculum. Yet the curriculum may not be highly rational in design, and many courses are not supported by a well-developed syllabus. Even with the existence of a carefully developed syllabus, it is the faculty member who must infuse the course with purpose and meaning.

Efforts to encourage institutions to clarify their mission and to state goals in precise operational terms are persistent but of modest yield. In spite of well-intentioned dedication, such attempts are typically only moderately successful, and the benefits generally are short-lived. The apparent failures do not stem from any necessary lack of expertness but relate directly to the intangible and complex nature of the academic task. Each student, for example, brings to the institution his own personal aspirations for the future and his own unique cluster of abilities, prior experiences, achievement, and growth potential. Faculty members are no less limited by their own experiences and competencies and cannot give to students or to the institution what they do not have.

As a result, colleges and universities have genuine difficulty in articulating their purposes. For good or ill, they have compensated for the lack of definition by delegating and decentralizing responsibility. Much of the authority for determining ends and means is delegated by the higher or central positions to the lower or operative levels. And, the larger and more complex the institution, the more significant delegation of authority and responsibility. Whether formally or by informal tacit agreement, academic departments and individual faculty members tend to participate heavily in setting institutional purposes and in determining the most effective means of achieving them. The content of courses, the nature of the curriculum, faculty work loads and schedules, and the selection, retention, and promotion of professional employees— these and other matters are strongly influenced by individual faculty members and by departmental action. The complexity of the academic task makes strong central control not only difficult but perhaps unwise. The bulk of the power and authority has been delegated to the academic department.

Academic Departments

The ascendancy of the department has paralleled the so-called knowledge explosion and the rise of the academic organization to a position of power in society. Academic departments are the principal organizational component of the university. Dressel, Johnson, and Marcus (1970) in their study of the department characterized the complex functions it performs: instructing and advising undergraduate majors; instructing undergraduate non-majors; instructing graduate students; advising or consulting with

101

professors from other disciplines; basic research; applied research; promoting the discipline within the university; promoting departmental views and interests in the college and the university; promoting the discipline and profession nationally; exploring interfaces of the disciplines; promoting career development of junior staff; attaining national recognition for the department; providing consultation services to business and industry and to governmental units; providing a scholarly and congenial environment in which to work; and providing a social and recreational network for those affiliated with the department.

The multifunctional character of the academic department is its most distinguishing quality in a comparison with the institute. Authority for defining the emphasis among functions is usually held by the chairman and by members of the departmental faculty. Despite its wide range of activities, the department is not functionally organized. The central focus is the discipline; the use to which the discipline is put—undergraduate or graduate instruction, basic or applied research, or programs of public service or continuing education—is another matter and not necessarily tied to the existence of the department.

Institutes and centers, as we stated earlier, tend to be organized around tasks or functions and to be multidisciplinary. Their range of functions is circumscribed. Most institutes, for example, may not engage in direct instruction of undergraduate students. A few, on the other hand, may *only* teach undergraduates. Still other institutes are set up solely for research and development, while others are directed toward public service. The contrast is between the open-ended, multifunctional mandate of departments and the typically restricted functions of institutes.

The position of the academic department within the organizational structure is reasonably predictable. Colleges or schools are composed of departments and the dean of the college usually reports directly to the central administrative structure of the university. No such uniformity is characteristic of institutes. They may be organized within departments or colleges; they may report, to an intermediate academic administrative officer; or they may be accountable directly to the president. The larger an institute, the more likely it is to float to the top of the institutional hierarchy.

Another significant difference between departments and institutes is the nature of their leadership. A mature academic department in a strong university is usually led by a chairman, who, while exercising certain clear administrative responsibilities and prerogatives, nonetheless tends to be a covener of the faculty, one who presides over departmental deliberations. The strong academic leader who shapes the department to conform with his own convictions and interests is the exception. Institutes, by contrast, have directors. Although they must be sensitive to the needs of professional personnel, including the need for basic academic freedoms and for adherence to a few generally accepted professional prerogatives, the distinction between the titles of chairman and director reflects real differences in role. Directors often directly shape goals and programs. Wtihout an a priori disciplinary definition of unity, the director must state and restate the purposes of the institute if he is to build a viable organizational identity and maintain a reasonable sense of purpose.

Institutes and centers are low men on the totem pole of power and status. Their power derives almost totally from an ability to provide access to research resources. There is no monopoly on this commodity, however, and in many institutions the great bulk of research support is channeled through the departmental and college structure. Nonetheless, for faculty members holding membership in both camps, affiliation with an institute can increase availability of resources.

The final distinction between institutes and departments relates to organizational and budgetary stability. The department tends to have a stable organization and its budget grows incrementally. Although growth in any given year may be minuscule, large fluctuations up or down are not common. The institute budget usually depends on external fund sources, and the size changes frequently. One year the director may be frantic in his search for staff; in another, he may be struggling to deal with an oversupply.

103

Beyond Academic Departments

Little wonder that faculty members in search of security and stability seek shelter in the academic department.

In short, institutes are different from departments and present a genuine organizational alternative. Whether they are considered to be positive additions to the structure depends on assumptions about fundamental purposes. If one understands the university to be functional, if not utilitarian, in character, institutes do add a useful dimension.

Institutes and Departments

University administrators and institute directors were asked to respond to a series of fifteen statements that set forth potential advantages of institutes. Their responses are shown in Table 8 in

Table 8

COMPARISONS OF ACADEMIC DEPARTMENTS AND INSTITUTES
BY UNIVERSITY ADMINISTRATORS AND INSTITUTE DIRECTORS

| | Percentage in Agreement | |
Questions	University Administrators	Institute Directors
Areas of Agreement		
1. Enable the university to establish new goals and respond to new constituencies more readily.	94	90
2. Make visible the university's commitment to a particular area of specialization.	89	89
3. Assemble interdisciplinary teams of faculty researchers more easily.	98	88
4. Generate financial support for the university's research function.	72	82
5. Allow a greater emphasis on applied, public service or problem oriented research.	63	67

104

Table 8 (cont.)

COMPARISONS OF ACADEMIC DEPARTMENTS AND INSTITUTES BY UNIVERSITY ADMINISTRATORS AND INSTITUTE DIRECTORS

	Percentage in Agreement	
Questions	University Administrators	Institute Directors
6. Allow a more rapid shift of university resources to meet new institutional responsibilities.	70	74
7. Allow for temporary restructuring of the university.	87	74
Areas of Difference		
8. Allow faculty members to pursue their careers in an optimum manner.	41	63
9. Allow more effective fiscal and management control of research programs.	33	57
10. Make available specialized personnel such as computer specialists and others.	41	53
11. Free faculty from the day to day schedule demands of teaching and committee assignments.	39	50
Areas of Joint Disagreement		
12. Provide better career advancement opportunities for younger staff members.	2	19
13. Assemble more and better research equipment.	33	50
14. Provide greater freedom for staff members to pursue their personal research interests.	41	50
15. Enable appraisal of junior staff members for possible subsequent tenured appointment to the faculty.	7	19

three major categories: statements which administrators and directors agreed were true; statements about which they did not agree with each other; and statements which both discounted or rejected as alleged advantages.

Directors and administrators—most of whom were academic or research vice-presidents or graduate deans—clearly agreed that institutes enable the university to establish new goals and respond to new constituencies more readily than do departments. Ninety per cent of the directors and 94 per cent of the administrators rated this advantage as a significant functional difference, suggesting that it is easier at times to influence the direction of university activities by creating new offices, bureaus, centers, and programs than by changing the goals, programs, and personnel of existing departments.

Closely related was the general agreement that institutes make visible the university's commitment to a particular area of specialization in a manner not possible in the department. Nine out of ten administrators and directors believed this to be the case, which perhaps explains the use of institutes by some "emerging universities" to gain increased recognition and enhance institutional prestige. Although several administrators and directors judged that departments are capable of emphasizing applied, public service, or problem-oriented research, approximately two-thirds of both groups ranked this capacity as an important advantage of institutes.

Also high on the list of agreements was the utility of institutes in assembling interdisciplinary teams. All but one administrator ranked this ability as an important advantage, and the great majority of directors agreed. Although the extent of interdisciplinary collaboration in institutes is sometimes exaggerated and not without problems, the difficulty of achieving significant collaboration within the conventional departmental structure makes the latter alternative even more remote.

Financial considerations were reflected in the belief shared by administrators (72 per cent) and directors (82 per cent) that institutes generate financial support for the university's research function which could not be generated by departments. There was the related belief, likely supportable by fact, that external sponsors, especially governments and foundations, are principally interested in funding problem-solving, task-oriented research. To the extent that these beliefs are substantiated, institutes should be in a position to attract grants and contracts which might otherwise be unavailable to the university.

Related to the area of management and finance was the general agreement that institutes more than departments allow a rapid shift of resources to meet new institutional responsibilities. This view was reinforced by the belief (reported earlier) that appointments to institutes are temporary. Also related are policies which prevent institutes from awarding tenure and which favor project-by-project funding rather than general institutional allocations as the principal means of support. Eighty-seven per cent of the administrators and nearly three-quarters of the directors also agreed that institutes enable temporary restructuring of the university in ways not possible in departments.

As might be expected, administrators and directors did not always see advantages and disadvantages alike. Directors believed their organizations to be superior in areas not necessarily endorsed by central administrators. Areas of general agreement seemed to dwell on the usefulness of institutes in shifting the goals as well as the resources of the university. Disagreements concentrated on the professional career advantages and disadvantages offered by institutes.

Institute directors thought, two to one, that institutes allow faculty members to pursue their careers in an optimum manner usually not possible within departments. About half of the directors claimed that a significant advantage of institutes is their ability to free faculty from the day-to-day schedule demands of teaching and committee assignments. Administrators tended to disagree on both counts. Nearly 60 per cent of the administrators implied that an institute is not necessarily an optimum spot for faculty members to pursue their careers, and essentially the same proportion refused to accept the view that institutes are able to free faculty from teaching and committee assignments to a greater degree than departments can.

The difference in views may stem from the different roles and institutional perspectives of the two groups. Obviously, the personal career choices of institute directors suggest that at least for them institutes met certain career needs that were not satisfied as fully in the conventional departmental structure. University administrators, on the other hand, having observed the very considerable growth in departmental power and autonomy, as well as the increase in faculty perquisites, status, and autonomy during the last decade, may have viewed the department as a nearly ideal spot from which to pursue a satisfying career.

Two additional areas of disagreement emerged. The first, relatively unimportant, is concerned with specialized personnel. Fifty-three per cent of the directors thought institutes made available specialized personnel such as computer specialists and other professionals difficult to employ in academic departments. Only 41 per cent of the administrators agreed, perhaps acknowledging that many departments do, in fact, employ specialized support personnel. The second area of disagreement was also probably related to different roles and perspectives: Two-thirds of the administrators rejected the view that institutes necessarily enable more effective fiscal and management control of research programs, but a majority of the institute directors, 57 per cent, felt that such control is stronger in institutes. In fact, performance controls and fiscal accountability to grantors may well be stronger in many institutes than in the typical academic department. The bureaucracy of the institute may be more conscious of mission, deadlines, budgets, and full reporting than most departments are. Questions of management control, on the other hand, can take several perspectives. University administrators could have had in view the direct relationships between institutes and their external sponsors and the sometimes weakened central administrative controls that result.

The judgments of university administrators and institute directors, however, were more likely to coincide than to differ.

Both groups essentially rejected significant functional advantages for institutes in four areas. Four out of five directors and 98 per cent of the administrators rejected the assertion that "research centers and institutes provide better career advancement opportunities for younger staff members than do academic departments." One reason for this opinion is suggested by the general agreement that institutes do not enable "appraisal of junior staff members for possible subsequent tenured appointment to the faculty more effectively than do academic departments." More than 80 per cent of the directors and more than 90 per cent of the administrators discounted tenure appraisal as an advantage. The career attractiveness of institutes is also diminished by their inability to control the reward structure, grant professorial rank, give promotions, award tenure, and provide other academic perquisites. Faculty members need to establish themselves in their discipline, especially if rewards are controlled by the discipline, so under existing arrangements younger scholars may need to be cautious in their affiliations with institutes.

Finally, directors and administrators agreed that institutes and centers do not necessarily assemble more and better research equipment than departments nor do they necessarily provide greater freedom for staff members to pursue their personal research interests. In each case, only half the directors and less than half of the administrators would claim these qualities as an advantage of institutes. In the first instance, many institutes have very little research equipment of their own but tend to rely on the laboratories and equipment of departments and of the university as a whole. In the second, freedom to pursue personal research interests can be greater in departments than in institutes, despite the very practical limitations placed on availability of research resources in departments. The compromise in institutes, in many instances, involves an adaptation in research interests in return for increased time and resources for research.

Overall, administrators and directors were in substantial agreement about the functional advantages and disadvantages of institutes. These units are found to be valuable primarily because they focus on tasks rather than disciplines and to increase flexibility, enabling the university to shift its resources and to adapt its structure to serve new goals and new constituencies. The advantages of this increased responsiveness are obvious. Its disadvantages, although less obvious, tend to follow the same dimensions. Flexibility creates instability. Recasting priorities, resources, and organizational structure inrceases conflict. And responsiveness to new goals and constituencies may modify institutional character and purposes in unintended directions. Certain disadvantages, such as instability, may be inherent in the institute model, but others, such as goal displacement, may reflect inadequate management control in complex universities. The principal point at issue is whether the institute model can or should be applied more generally in American higher education and, if so, how its liabilities can be minimized and its assets developed and exploited.

Controversy and Criticism

Institutes have generated criticisms and complaints far out of proportion to their numbers. One recent critic observed: "On a rough guess, I should think at least 75 per cent of all existing institutes, centers and bureaus in the academic sphere of the university should be phased out" (Nesbet, 1971, p. 219). Many observers believe that institutes not only fail to make a positive contribution but are the chief culprits in an alleged prostitution of the purposes of the American university. One of the most common complaints is that institutes, with their programs of sponsored research and public service, have undermined teaching. Nesbet suggests a need to clear the scene. "There cannot be any honoring of teaching so long as there is left in existence the whole, vast structure of research-dominated—especially large-scale, research-dominated —institutes and centers that tower above all else in the university today . . . . Until this thick overgrowth is cleared, it is difficult to see how the function of teaching can again become an honored one on the American campus" (pp. 224–225)'.

A corollary charge is that institutes have weakened the

department by syphoning off the time, loyalties, and talents of faculty which would otherwise be wholly devoted to its work. Moreover, conflict can result from a dual system of rewards in which departmental faculty members with appointments in an institute appear to receive disproportionate support for research and scholarly activity while faculty members employed only in the department not only are left with less support for research but believe they carry heavier teaching loads as part of the bargain.

Some of the bitterest critics say institutes have weakened the authority structure in the university. The principal offender here is the joint appointment, an alleged fragmentation of faculty effort in two or more units, and the accompanying problems of coordination, community, and equity. Faculty members employed jointly in institutes and departments sometimes receive perquisites not available to their colleagues employed solely in the department or solely in the institute. A favor denied in one quarter sometimes is granted in another. Judgments by chairmen and directors on salary increases, promotion, tenure, and merit can differ. The fundamental fear expressed by some is that institutes weaken the authority of the department chairman and the senior members of the faculty and, in so doing, weaken the authority of the university to exert necessary controls on a wide range of crucial personnel matters.

Those concerned with tidiness in the academic community criticize institutes and centers for their apparent fragmentation of the structure. Complex as the typical university may be with as many as a hundred or more academic departments distributed among a dozen or more colleges, the introduction of thirty, forty, or perhaps as many as one hundred institutes distributed at random throughout the hierarchy further contributes to the sense of disorganization. Added to this is the confusion introduced by lack of standardized terms such as institute, center, bureau, and so forth. By and large, the distinctions and usage are inconsistent and arbitrary.

One of the most basic criticisms is the rejection of the purposes institutes and centers have been created to serve. Many within the academic community do not accept their functions as appropriate to the mission of the university. A related factor is the alleged introduction of a "knowledge for profit" motive. Jacques Barzun (1968), in his statement on *The American University*, describes the academic rat race:

> *The scholar, almost in proportion to his capacity for juggling claims, soon realizes that he must exert himself harder and harder to maintain the same output. Such is the natural result of modern communications: as consultant to one firm, he attracts the notice of three others, which write him alluring offers. In Washington, his success with one project leads to his becoming a referee on others; within the profession, his discoveries suggest that a group of fellow workers should start a new journal. He must be the editor and see whether it cannot be housed in his university. Meanwhile, right there at home and unknown to him, notable men in different disciplines have come to the conclusion that the world requires the immediate study of a neglected subject— say, the social impact of science. Nothing less than a new institute will accomplish this, as the work is interdisciplinary. Our man is approached, he is interested, he has connections. Before he knows it, he is writing prospectuses, haggling with the university office of projects and grants about proposed budgets, sitting through meetings where the word* angle *in the first draft is thoughtfully changed to* approach *and back again [p. 22].*

This kind of opportunistic orientation to the academic marketplace, the searching after grants, the lending of oneself to the highest bidder—these are the qualities to which many object and for which they hold institutes responsible. Scholarship for profit, it is alleged, has debased university purposes and contributed substantially to the confidence crisis and confusion over purpose in which many universities now find themselves.

Criticisms of institutes are numerous and persistent. Some critics see the university in a purest state, unrelated to functional,

112

utilitarian, or societal purposes. Others wish to turn back the clock, to bring back the more tranquil good old days when times were simpler and purposes more circumscribed. Still others seek the ideal university, and for many who seek this ideal higher education institution, institutes would not be part of their utopian design.

Critics often ignore the fact that the contemporary university has changed largely at the direction of the society that supports it and the academic men who run it. Although the teaching of undergraduate students was the principal purpose of most universities prior to World War II, they now carry on a wide array of functions that extend far beyond this initial conception. Charges that institutes have weakened academic departments are hard to take seriously in view of the astounding rise in power and influence of the department during the last two decades. While it may be true that institutes and centers have modified the power and authority structure, the redistribution has had positive as well as negative effects.

Charges of a fragmented academic community, however, remain largely unanswered. Clearly, institutes are not well integrated with the university's organizational structure. On most campuses, institutes have grown rapidly, apart from the basic academic plan of the institution, and on a largely opportunistic and pragmatic basis; the result is a bewildering spider's network of organizational relationships. Though the lack of a grand design has made possible experimentation with new relationships and structures, the time may be at hand when most universities will want to draw from the best of their experiences and bring greater order in the development and management of institutes.

Coming to Grips with Issues

Both opponents and advocates agree that institutes often exist outside the central life of the university. Opponents see them as autonomous, opportunistic, and distorting basic university goals and purposes. Advocates, especially those involved in the day to day

113

work, see institutes as isolated, disenfranchised, and exploited. Some of the conflict in views stems from a general lack of understanding of institutes as an alternative to the department, an alternative that should complement the department but neither mimic nor replace it.

At least five major issues must be resolved by colleges and universities as they attempt to integrate institutes and centers more fully than they have been. First, and clearly the most important of these issues, is the relationship between the goals and purposes of the institute and university objectives. Numerous instances can be cited in which institute goals were at cross-purposes with those of the parent university. The mere existence of an external funding source and the excuse that "no university monies are involved" can no longer serve as an alibi. Classified research is only one aspect of this issue. Universities must periodically evaluate and appraise institute performance and devise some orderly mechanism for ensuring that its activities do indeed accord with broad institutional purposes. Moreover, the academic community at large and university administrators in particular must play a more active role than they presently do in shaping the goal structure of institutes to guard against the charge of goal displacement resulting from an overly opportunistic pursuit of external fund sources.

The appropriate placement of institutes in the organization must also be decided. The basic issue here, again, is who controls whom. Some universities have initiated programs to bring all institutes within colleges and departments. Others have moved in the opposite direction, removing all these units from control of academic departments and colleges. The fundamental question is which set of values will prevail. If institutes are placed within the departmental and college structure, one must expect that the fundamental values of the discipline or profession will eventually reign. If one separates institutes from the direct control of departments and colleges, appropriate systems of academic control, either within or analogous to those exercised on most campuses through university senates, must be constructed to ensure that these units are brought within the decision-making and control mechanisms of the institution.

Institutes and the University

The third major issue is the future of institutes and centers as scarce financial resources continues to decrease on many campuses. What will happen when the crunch comes? Will resources be taken away from departments and colleges to support sagging institute budgets? Are the limited new monies available to the institution to be channeled disproportionately to support those institutes in financial stress? And if these funds are not used to support institutes and centers, on what basis is this decision reached? If institutes are genuinely attuned to institutional goals and purposes, should they not share proportionately in available resources? Should not institutes be relieved of some of the necessity of living from hand to mouth from the academic marketplace? These questions, of course, are affected by the extent to which various constituencies, particularly state legislators and statewide coordinating boards, understand institute functions to be not only legitimate but necessary.

Many universities must also confront the issue of full legitimization of nonteaching functions as a component in university goals. Although many universities profess a triumvirate of purposes —teaching, research, and service—organizational structures have been designed principally to carry out the teaching function. Specifically, departments are best suited to instruct undergraduate and graduate majors and to carry out "departmental" research. If the university indeed does pursue three major objectives, what further refinement of the organizational structure is needed to accommodate the full range of purposes?

The final issue to be addressed is the present dual system of professional personnel policies applied to faculty members employed in academic departments and to those professionals employed only in institutes. Many good arguments can be heard in defense of the status quo, but the basic question remains: Which benefits, essential to those who labor in departments, are somehow not needed by those employed in institutes? Tenure, promotion, and other faculty personnel policies are under review at many universities, and such reexamination should inquire into the possibility of reducing the present inconsistencies and inequities.

115

VIII

Conclusions and Recommendations

The ultimate role of institutes and centers in the university is undecided, but unquestionably it will differ among institutions. Despite their shortcomings, institutes have added a structural alternative and a contrasting dimension to the organizational configuration. They enable higher education institutions to accept new responsibilities and pursue them in new ways. How to strengthen their contributions and diminish their weaknesses is the primary task. Within this context ways to improve the functioning of the whole university may also be found.

Summary of Findings

A combination of forces—societal, professional, and institutional—contributed to the rapid growth of institutes and centers. The growing dependence of society on scientific and technological innovation and the related influx of foundation, industrial, and government funds unquestionably were critical factors. Money available for research and development increased dramatically. Much of the increased support was based on a strong utilitarian or problem-solving motive which required a different orientation by

116

universities and a somewhat less rigid defense of disciplinary boundaries. New ways of organizing and relating professional personnel were also necessary; the professorial independence of individual faculty decreased somewhat in favor of coordinated team efforts.

Concurrent with the proliferation of institutes was a growth in academic professionalism that emphasized the importance of creating knowledge rather than merely transmitting it. More and more, institutions required faculty to demonstrate competence through evidence of publication and national reputation. These practices, in turn, contributed to the ascendency of the research function and to the emergence of institutes as instruments useful to the faculty in satisfying professional career needs.

For other faculty members, institutes offered career satisfactions not otherwise available and perquisites, such as secretarial help, travel, and time for research. Not all faculty members, of course, found these attractions persuasive, and majority faculty support for the establishment of an institute was rare. This goal was still achieved with the sanction of a critical mass of faculty members, preferably led by a capable scholar-entrepreneur, who could articulate the goals to be served by the institute, devise and communicate the efficacy of the means to achieve those ends, and mobilize the essential support both inside and outside the university.

Institutes and centers did not originate entirely as a result of the utilitarian aims of external sponsors or the career ambitions of faculty members. Institutional concerns were also important. The desire of faculty to initiate, direct, or be a part of institutes made these units helpful to administrators trying to recruit and retain able faculty members. Administrators also used them as instruments to strengthen graduate education and increase research productivity. Problems of communication and coordination among departments led some administrators to view institutes as useful in coping with these enigmas. And although some generated their share of conflict, institutes were also used by some university administrators to resolve conflicts, to separate warring factions, or to otherwise keep peace within the academy.

117

Beyond Academic Departments

University administrators approved proposals to create new institutes not only because they might help the institution do better the things it was already doing, but in the hope that the new institute might take on new tasks, serve new constituencies, in new ways, with greater effectiveness. For some universities, institutes apparently held out the prospects of greatness. Self-conscious of a modest academic standing, some administrators saw in institutes the chance to increase institutional visibility and prestige, while others attempted departmental reform by creating institutes.

Obviously, not all forces operated in each instance, and some factors were more significant in certain universities than in others. The principal impetus for establishing institutes in some institutions came almost exclusively from the faculty, while in others initiative derived primarily from members of the administration. Yet nearly all successfully established and operating institutes met minimum criteria: They addressed a societal need; university administrative concurrence was given; and a core of faculty members was committed to bring the institute into being.

The functions carried out by institutes are usually more restricted than those of departments, and much of the special utility of institutes and the bulk of their special contribution to the organizational configuration stem from these more specific and limited functional definitions. Any of the three functions normally associated with the mission of complex universities may be performed by institutes, but a single unit rarely has an unlimited mandate to perform all activities. More commonly, it is restricted to one or two functions; whereas academic departments usually have broad assignments to provide undergraduate and graduate instructional programs, carry out research, and engage in public service.

How an institute does its work also is circumscribed. Some institutes directly perform the function—teaching, research, or public service. Others are designed specifically to administer and coordinate performance. And still other institutes facilitate the activities of other units. Libraries, for example, perhaps the oldest form of a special purpose center, facilitate the teaching and research of others. Computer centers are created principally to aid, not to

118

perform, teaching and research. The nature and extent of institute limitations can be illustrated by a functional matrix relating the three types of functions and the three ways of addressing those functions. No institute claiming to perform all nine combinations of functions was identified. The mission of most institutes was restricted principally to one or two combinations, such as the performance of research, the administration of public service, or the facilitation of instruction and research.

The fact that many professional staff members employed by institutes are engaged in a broad range of activities reflects the need for career satisfactions beyond those available in centers. This variety may also be related to career expectations for faculty members and the assumption that each should demonstrate successful performance in all three functional areas. In most cases, these career needs are met through joint appointments to departments and institutes, but when such appointments are not practical or possible, it is not uncommon for institute staff members to contribute their time to departments in return, for example, for the opportunity to teach.

There are understandable pressures to broaden the functions of institutes. Opportunities for increased career satisfactions for institute staff members and the organizational stability and security that come from having broadly stated missions present genuine attractions. Such expansion, however, would tend to minimize the special functional qualities of institutes and diminish their significance as an alternative to the departmental organizational form. It may be necessary and desirable to expand the mandate of selected institutes, but their status thus becomes akin to that of a department or school.

The ability of institutes to bring about interdisciplinary collaboration is an important but perhaps overemphasized function. Three different modes of collaboration were identified. Faculty members from several different disciplines, for example, may work together on a single project, carry out the research as a team, and develop a single integrated report of their findings. Or faculty members from several disciplines may work independently on separate aspects of a larger problem. In a third model, faculty members from a single discipline, working as a team, may call on persons from another discipline or disciplines to give supplementary assistance as required. All three models of collaboration are widely applied, although institutes in the physical and life sciences apparently use the first model more extensively than do others.

Few institute directors claimed that all their programs were interdisciplinary, and most institutes in the physical and life science and social science-humanities groups reported a comparatively small number of different disciplines represented on their professional staffs. Water center directors did not claim a great deal of collaboration, but, in fact, more departments and disciplines were represented on their staffs than on those of the other two categories. The critical factor in institute functioning is not collaboration, per se, and the number of disciplines involved, but the ability to coordinate the talents of several professionals in accomplishing a single task or goal.

Institute organizational models fall along a continuum defined by two extremes: One is characterized by a stable budget and by a centrally officed staff which is employed on a continuing basis and which maintains primary ties and professional identity within the institute; in the other, professional staff members are employed largely on a part-time temporary basis and have offices in as well as professional ties and identity with their academic departments. The institute has little permanently assigned space, an irregular budget, and little equipment.

Three general types of institutes were identified along this continuum and the principal differences among the three were traced to differences in the stability of goals, programs, and resources. Standard institutes resembled the typical bureaucratic organization. Goals and budget levels were relatively stable, and program activities were reasonably predictable. As a result, personnel, space, and equipment requirements also tended to be comparatively secure. Adaptive institutes faced somewhat different conditions. Their goals, program activities, and rate of resource consumption were less predictable, and consequently personnel and space demands were less stable. Adaptive institutes were more likely to use part-time and temporary personnel, to have decentralized office space, and to shift their programs to meet changes in resources and the varying needs of their clients. At the far end of the continuum were what might be called *shadow institutes*—hard to find and, once identified, sometimes rejected as being merely paper institutes without substance. Their directors, typically, worked part-time; their staffs, budgets, and facilities frequently were nonexistent. As organizations, they appeared at times to be figments of faculty fantasy. Their dormant state and their lack of commitment to a particular ongoing program, however, did provide a latent network of talent that could be activated to meet new needs should they arise. In the current form, shadow institutes can provide the university with a low-cost option of maintaining an organizational capability that might be brought to life in time of need. Too frequently, however, these institutes were products of faculty chimera or administrative timidity.

The three types carry assets as well as liabilities. The adaptive and shadow institute models offer an alternative to the conventional bureaucratic organizational form, provide greater operating flexibility, and enhance the application of newer management techniques such as program planning budgeting systems. Standard institutes, on the other hand, conform to conventional expectations about what organizations should be and provide their clients with greater assurance of stability and time-proven reliability. Staff members in the standard model may be more secure and have greater career satisfactions. Perhaps for these reasons, directors of the two flexible models frequently strive to increase stability in their organizations and, in time, to transform them into standard institutes.

Although institutes and centers are sometimes referred to as autonomous, much of the control over goals, programs, and personnel rests outside the institute with grantors and academic departments. Although the organizational structure of the complex university has changed with the advent of institutes, power, the ability to control rewards and sanctions, remains principally in academic departments. Most institutes may appoint professional personnel outside the departmental and college structure, but comparatively few such appointments are made except in the largest, most heavily research-oriented universities.

Most institute staff members hold joint appointments in academic departments. Professorial titles, access to tenure, and participation in governance frequently are available only through departmental appointment. Such appointments, however, often give departments power to influence important personnel matters such as promotions and salary increases. And, significantly, the need to provide a joint appointment as inducement allows departments to control the initial recruitment of institute staff members, to grant favors, and to "discipline" when necessary.

Departments also exercise controls through formal and informal assessment of institutes. Some universities require formal periodic evaluations of institute programs and accomplishments. Representatives from academic departments or the faculty senate (typically open only to department-affiliated faculty) may be called upon to conduct the review. Moreover, on an informal basis, carefully placed comments within and beyond the institution can subtly shape opinions and professional judgments about the quality of institute accomplishments.

Yet institutes, not without their own power and influence, tend to hold their own. Access to increased financial support for research, released time from departmental teaching duties, employment opportunities during the summer months, and travel funds may be provided. Department chairmen can expand the breadth and depth of their staffs, solve certain departmental financial and management problems, find employment for graduate students, and meet other departmental needs through cooperation with institutes. If one were to distinguish between power and its more informal counterpart influence, one might suggest that institutes exercise considerable influence within the university authority structure but that the power rests principally in the departments.

Though many institutes have advisory committees, they are used primarily to maintain satisfactory working relations and to

resolve conflicts between the institute and other units and constituents inside and outside the university. Institutes are vulnerable
to a variety of pressures from grantors, external constituent groups,
academic departments, professional staff members, university administrators, and others. Advisory committees are useful mechanisms
for identifying conflict and managing these pressures. Committees
are usually composed of academic or external power figures such
as deans and department chairmen, state agency officials, and
other official representatives from constituent groups. Few professors
and scientists who do not also hold significant administrative positions are members. Some committees play a low-keyed, general
advisory role, and in a significant number of instances the advisory
committee was openly reported to be nonfunctional. Many water
center directors attributed a significant role to their committees, but
other institutes tended to rate the program and policy influence of
the committee quite low. No instance was found in which the committee was reported to play a strong governance or decision-making
role.

The strongest influence in shaping institute programs is
apparently the institute director, suggesting that effective academic
leadership, important in all sectors of the university, may be especially important in institutes and centers. The substitution of a task
or problem orientation for a disciplinary orientation, the need for
highly coordinated teamwork, and the frequent need to make rapid
shifts in goals and program resources require strong leadership. And
directors often must generate a significant measure of their financial
support from external, and not necessarily recurring, sources. In
contrast to the department chairman, the director is more likely to
be an academic entrepreneur, capable of relating to foundation
officers, government officials, and industrial executives as well as
to his colleagues, and willing to assume a considerable measure of
personal responsibility for the survival and prosperity of the institute. Accepting these responsibilities, the director also tends to exercise increased power and influence in institute programs and
policies.

When comparing institutes and academic departments institute directors and university administrators agreed that institutes enable the university to establish new goals and respond to new constituencies; shift resources to meet new responsibilities; temporarily restructure the institution; provide greater visibility for areas of institutional specialization. Both also believed that institutes more than departments were effective in assembling interdisciplinary teams; allowed the institution to emphasize applied public service or problem-oriented research; and were effective in generating additional financial support. Administrators and directors had some doubts about the institute as an optimum location for faculty career development. The overwhelming majority of respondents concluded that institutes do not present better career advancement opportunities for younger staff members than departments do. Perhaps this conclusion was related to the conviction, also held by both groups of respondents, that institutes do not enable appraisal of junior staff members for possible subsequent tenured appointments as effectively as do departments.

Recommendations

What recommendations can be advanced to strengthen the role of institutes and centers in the university, to minimize the negative aspects experienced in the past, and enhance their contribution to the total effectiveness of the institution? The following six recommendations are drawn from the context of this study.

First, universities should devote more attention to the nature of institute programs and accomplishments and make sure that the character of each institute is congruent with that of the university. Many observers have viewed the growth of institutes as overly opportunistic, too responsive to the whims of governments and foundations, too eager to seek additional money—regardless of the purpose and the strings attached. Too frequently the judgment of academic entrepreneurs may be a substitute for the criteria of institutional purpose. Proposed curriculum changes and new degree programs are subjected to an almost endless series of reviews and are judged in terms of need, cost, and alignment with the institu-

124

tion's mission. But a multimillion-dollar research or service program can pass through most institutional councils with little delay if the budget page shows an appropriate calculation of overhead costs. While this lack of scrutiny has enabled institutes to respond to new constituencies and to address important purposes that otherwise might have been disallowed, it has also contributed to an inability of universities to control and defend their purposes. As a result, institutes are seen by many as serving private ends, or, as Paul Dressel and associates (1969) charged, "The basic difficulty is that universities have come to be dominated by their professors rather than by their purposes" (p. 24).

The task of relating institute proposals to institutional purposes is not easy. Institutional purposes are pluralistic, sometimes conflicting, and invariably difficult to define. As a result, the criteria against which proposals for new institutes and programs can be judged are weak and ill defined. Some statements suggest that the principal basis for judgment is the extent to which an institute would serve some secondary interest of departments, faculty members, or graduate students. It is apparently difficult to get at the more intangible questions of overall mission, society's needs, and the likely contribution of institute programs toward these ends.

The argument is sometimes advanced that as long as an external agency will finance a given program, the fine points of merit need not be debated, for it actually costs the institution nothing. Analysis of institute budgets, however, suggests that nearly all receive institutional core support, usually in the range of 20 to 33 per cent, and that the larger the amount of funds from external sources, the larger the institution's core contribution. Moreover, programs require space; they consume the talents of people; they broaden and complicate the task of administrative leadership; and indeed in the aggregate they can change the character of the institution. Thus, no institute or institute program is without its costs. The highest institutional costs, as has been demonstrated on some campuses with large weapons research funding, may occur in programs in which the directly calculable expenditures appear to be the least. The important issue is the program's congruence with

125

the institutional mission, and this relationship should be established by the university itself—not by external agencies or by selected academic entrepreneurs.

Some institutions have attempted to frame criteria against which such judgments can be made. One set, developed by the University of California (1968, p. 6), is as follows: (1) scholarly productivity associated with the institute; (2) number of graduate students meaningfully associated with the institute; (3) extent to which the institute creates an interdepartmental or interdisciplinary meeting group; (4) ease of finding a new director within the group when the occasion arises; (5) nature and amount of external funding; (6) extent to which the institute fosters graduate education; (7) service to the state and nation. Though such criteria are a marked advancement over the norm in most universities and suggest some critical issues, they concentrate too heavily on secondary by-products, such as employment of graduate students and the amount of external funding. Too little attention is given to the major substantive issues of institutional and institute mission and social need.

The following questions suggest criteria that might address these somewhat more intangible issues. Are the proposed programs and the general character of the institute congruent with broadly defined institutional goals and purposes? Would approval of a new institute or new program proposals contribute to or enhance the operational definition of mission? How does the proposed institute or program relate to the needs of society? Is its social purpose one the university would wish to defend and advance? If serving such a purpose is beyond the traditional institutional mission, should goals be reconceived and updated to incorporate these social ends?

What resources are needed, not only in terms of budget, but in terms of space, time, human talents, and other requirements? Are the social and institutional priorities sufficient to merit this investment of resources in preference to other alternative allocation patterns? What are the implications of the proposed institute or program for changing the nature of the institution? Recognizing

Conclusions and Recommendations

that institutional character is not static, would approval of this institute or program shape it in desirable directions?

Suggestions that universities should be less opportunistic, devote more attention to the relevance of program proposals, and and cause decisions on priorities to be made inside rather than outside the institution are not new in any sense. The failure to respond to these admonitions stems partly from a lack of clarity and an absence of agreement on institutional purposes. Some argue that a university should not strive for a neatly defined mission. Even when definitions are made they are frequently so broad as to appear relatively useless as guides to specific decisions. And the means of relating institute proposals and programs to institutional purposes are nearly always inadequate. Who defines purposes, suggests priorities, and accepts the burden for saying "yes" or "no"? Perhaps more important than "who" is "how"—through what means and mechanisms are such decisions to be made?

If universities are to gain greater control over their purposes and make decisions about institutes in other than the simplest terms, new decision-making mechanisms need to be established to ensure agreement between institute and university purposes. Campus-wide review councils, open hearings, different funding patterns by the federal government and foundations, more sophisticated institutional planning, and more careful review of institute programs by central administrative officers are a few of the options. The appropriate mechanisms will vary among institutions, but certainly the opportunistic, uncoordinated, externally guided growth of institutes and their programs must give way to a more carefully reasoned, rationally planned, and institutionally defensible pattern of development. Such a shift will be essential not only in evaluating new programs and proposals but in merging, phasing out, or terminating institutes whose functions have been accomplished or which have low priority. The dangers of the more careful review and scrutiny are that proposals for change may become hopelessly bogged down in debate and in defense of the status quo. There are many reasons to question the ability of universities to make the tough reviews required to bring institute and university purposes into line, but the costs of failing to do so, now apparent after two decades of uncontrolled growth, may be higher than most institutions can or should pay.

Second, we recommend that university policy relating to personnel matters, such as title, promotion, benefits, and perquisites, should be uniform, regardless of the specific division in which the professional person is employed or the functions he performs. Some will take exception to the suggestion that personnel policies should be reexamined with a view toward diminishing the differences. On campuses where institutes and centers are well accepted, one can argue that a major reason for this harmony is the evolved-through-experience reservation of tenure granting and other privileges to departments. In addition, a case can be made that tenure and the title of professor should be reserved for those who "profess." Beyond these somewhat philosophical considerations are the practical problems of making continuing commitments on soft money.

Such dual policies, however, reflect certain inconsistencies which, while explainable in terms of tradition and pragmatic utility, may be increasingly difficult to apply and defend. Problems are minimized in some institutions by making sure that all or nearly all professionals have access to the "preferred" policies through departmental affiliation. On campuses where institutes are still few and relatively small these tactics work with only occasional strain and inequity. But in institutions that rely heavily on institutes which may be larger than the departments with which professional staff members are or would be affiliated, the picture is quite different.

The results of dual policies are evident in interpersonal inequities and apparent feelings of second-class status, in low morale among professional institute staff, and in feelings of separateness and isolation. Movement of personnel among university divisions and functions is retarded because faculty members want to gain or maintain access to the preferred sector. Those who split their appointments between the two camps frequently find that significant decisions regarding their future—on rank, promotion, tenure—may not be made jointly, but principally, if not solely, by the academic department.

These problems apply differently to different institutions. A few universities have only a few institutes, and for them the difficulties are still comparatively minor. But for universities with nearly as many institutes as departments and for universities that wish to make increased use of the institute as an organizational form, greater equity in personnel policies may be essential. Specific areas for institutional review include appointment and promotion policies; participation in institutional governance and decision-making, including membership or representation in institutionwide governing bodies; fringe benefits, including policies on retirement policies and sabbatical leaves; equity in job security and academic freedom, with essentially common standards applied universitywide regardless of the sector of employment or source of funds.

Implementation of a consistent policy will undoubtedly result in new problems and issues. Universities now take substantial risks in seeking and accepting external grant funds because institute staffs can be cut sharply in times of economic emergency. Recent experience has demonstrated, however, that such flexibility may be equally essential across the institution—for departments as well as institutes. A shift toward a single policy for all professional personnel would also modify the power relationships within academic departments and between departments and institutes. Faculty members, for example, would not necessarily have to hold membership in a department in order to gain access to special employment perquisites, and departments would have fewer controls over institute staff. The quality controls now exercised by departments would also be loosened, and new ones would need to be devised, preferably for the whole institution and applied so as to enhance consistency in policies and to ease the transfer of professional staff between departments and institutes.

Our third recommendation is that the special structural and functional characteristics of institutes should be preserved and their utility as complementary organizational units enhanced. We have described these special attributes as task orientation, flexible goals and structure, and restricted functional mandate. Many of the alleged special advantages of institutes and centers stem directly from these organizational qualities. Arguments that institutes should be allowed to increase their functions, to concentrate their resources on teaching, research, and public service in a broad general problem area, occasionally have merit and result, in effect, in the creation of a new professional school. But wholesale transformations would destroy their unique contribution to the university organizational configuration.

Broad functional mandates are attractive to those in institutes. Authorization to engage in a wide range of activities can contribute to security, enable professional staff members to obtain a range of career satisfactions, and permit directors to expand significantly their base of operations. Yet if institute goals were viewed as relatively permanent, if most professional staff members saw their relationship with the institute as stable and continuing, if the institute were allowed to engage in instruction, research, and public service however it wished and to operate under a set of uniform professional personnel policies, the institute would become simply another academic department. Failure to retain the restricted, task-oriented focus of institutes would decrease the usefulness of institutes as complementary organizational forms and as alternatives to the departmental structure.

Fourth, we believe policies and procedures should be established for effective and systematic review of institute programs and proposals, with a major review to be conducted at least once every five years. Few organizations relish the prospect of being evaluated. Survival is a very basic instinct whether applied to human beings or the organizations to which they belong, and institutes do not often dissolve gracefully at the conclusion of their tasks. Nor, perhaps, should they. Early definitions of mission tend to change, and regular reappraisals and redefinitions are appropriate. Shifts in emphasis, however, too frequently tend to be governed by the market—by what sponsors are willing to buy—and not by systematic review and evaluation. Such market-oriented shifts contribute to goal displacement, in which an institute reverses the priority between its goals and its means and the winning of the contract becomes the only real goal.

To look at the problem from another perspective, many universities have placed enrollment ceilings on the institution as a whole or on specific programs. Changes in the birth rate and college-attendance patterns suggest a comparatively stable enrollment picture in future years. With such static conditions, should proposals for new institutes and centers be weighed solely in terms of the merit and effectiveness of their programs or from the point of view of the overall balance of programs within the institution? If a proposal is approved, are there old institutes, departments, or colleges that could be phased out? Social needs change and institutional priorities shift, but the mechanisms for ensuring that university programs are responsive to these changes are weak and often controlled by outside forces.

The review and evaluation of departmental as well as institute goals, programs, and accomplishments should be more systematic, careful, and effective than they are at present. Each institute should receive a formal review at least once every five years by a committee, appointed by the president of the university, including representatives from the university administration, the constituents served, the faculty, and the institute itself. Committee recommendations might take various forms. In nearly all cases, recommendations for improvement might be expected. Changes in emphasis and new alternatives, directions, and priorities should be examined. Merger with another university unit, broadening or narrowing its scope of operations, fresh leadership, and even the possibility of phasing out all or portions of institute operations should be included among the alternatives.

University administrators have been reluctant to deal with these issues. Advisory committees typically have had neither the mandate nor the disposition to initiate significant reviews. And institute directors are conscious of the need for organizational survival and stability. Nonetheless, the times will demand much more careful review and evaluation of programs and priorities in all sectors of universities. Large numbers of institutes now operate on most campuses. Growing pressure will force them to respond to new needs and new constituencies and to weed out obsolete programs.

Fifth, increased attention should be given to the integration of institutes with the university in terms of organization, communication, physical facilities, and governance. Evidence of the lack of assimilation is abundant. Institute directors and staff members, for example, frequently complain that they are apparently outside the normal communication networks and do not receive many of the ordinary universitywide communications that somehow bombard other members of the faculty. The physical facilities of institutes are sometimes located on the periphery of the campus, contributing to the feelings of separateness and isolation. University planning efforts frequently ignore institutes and concentrate on departments and colleges. Separate personnel policies and separate governance patterns also contribute to poor integration.

The problem of bringing institutes into the university is partly organizational and partly attitudinal, but principally it is a policy problem. The structural aspect is perhaps most easily solved. Several universities have established umbrella organizations to coordinate and administer the programs of a series of smaller institutes. For example, at The Pennsylvania State University, the Institute for Science and Engineering serves as a general organizational unit for several institutes and centers. No single design would be appropriate in all or even most instances, but institutions should reexamine their general structures in order to strengthen the ties between institutes and the university as a whole.

Much of the feeling of separateness among institute staff results not merely from organizational isolation but from prevailing attitudes that institutes are somehow autonomous, chartered to define their own mission since they are supported in large part by funds from external sponsors and are responsive to external constituencies. Moreover, they engage in tasks and functions historically not given heavy emphasis within the university. It is not surprising, therefore, that many institutes have not really been embraced as integral parts of the university. Steps can and should be taken to bring about closer integration. As personnel policies are reevaluated and made equitable across the institution and as institute programs are appraised and reaffirmed in terms of institutional purpose and character, considerable progress can be made. And as the organizational structure of the university is modified to embrace the institutes, the attitudes as well as the fact of organizational isolation should change.

Finally, we recommend that colleges and universities make increased use of institutes and centers as organizational alternatives to academic departments in areas of instruction as well as research and public service. The prospect of more institutes may be an anathema to some skeptics. The times, however, call for a searching reexamination of all aspects of academic life, including the very organization of the university itself. In advancing such a possibility, we are reminded of the appropriate caution advanced by Orlans (1972). "The thirst for organizational solutions to enduring human problems—perhaps derived from the effective organization of industrial production and distribution—can lead to an overevaluation of research and research institutes. We should not expect from knowledge more than we can expect from men" (p. 180). And we should also not expect from organizational structure more than we can expect from men. Nonetheless, there is reason to look closely at further applications of the institute model as universities attempt to modernize their organizational structure.

Several concerns underlie the suggestion that institutes might be more widely used than they now are—not to replace but to supplement the academic department. One of the most obvious present challenges is that of sheer numbers. Universities that once enrolled fewer than ten thousand students now enroll more than twenty or thirty thousand. But enrollment tells only part of the story of radical increase in institutional operations. The number of functions served has grown, and the resources devoted to research, development, and service have escalated. Terms such as the multiversity have been coined to describe the changes in scale that have come about. More recently, requests have been made to decentralize universities and higher education systems, to increase options and variety, and to create a stronger "sense of society" within large, impersonal institutions.

Calls for decentralization apparently ignore the fact that many current problems stem not so much from excessive central control as from institutional fragmentation, unintended decentralization, and lack of coordination. The departments, organized around disciplines rather than tasks, require a high degree of coordination. Single tasks, such as the education of undergraduate students, are split among different departments and offices. As students advance to upper-division and graduate work, concentration in the discipline tends to increase and the problem of cross-departmental coordination decreases. At the lower-division level, however, the structure requires a degree of interdepartmental and interstaff coordination not easily achieved in large, complex universities.

One key to decentralization is to reduce dependence among various operating units and to delegate increased authority and responsibility for a single task to one unit. If universities are to decentralize, they must redefine tasks and modify their organizational structures so that subunits require little coordination. Institutes have accomplished this objective in the area of research, gathering researchers from several different disciplines with varied skills and coordinating a single, complex task. The same organizational model might also be applied to improving undergraduate instruction by bringing together several of the now separate components essential to the task.

The problem of whether to organize by task or specialty (discipline) is not unique to higher education. Business and industrial groups must also decide whether to protect the integrity of the several kinds of professional competence or to organize into project units and thereby mobilize the different skills required for a specific job. With the exception of institutes and centers and a limited number of experimental and cluster colleges, however, higher education institutions have seldom experimented with task-oriented structures. The urge toward professionalism and the unquestioned adherence to professional or disciplinary values have tended to wed

134

most institutions to the departmental model. The expansion of institutional roles and functions and the massive increases in scale of operations have been accommodated principally by expanding role definitions and expectations for faculty members and their departments rather than through shifts in the organizational configuration.

More than a decade ago, Litchfield (1959) advanced the notion that colleges and universities need to establish "flexibility of faculty organizational structure as an objective" (p. 356). The very definition of the task might enable an institution to sharpen the operational definition of its mission and to strengthen the bonds between institutional function and organizational structure now largely obliterated.

A related reason for considering expanded use of the institute form is the persistent call for more diversity in higher education programs, for more options, and less homogeneity (Newman, 1971; Martin, 1969; Carnegie Commission on Higher Education, 1971). The conventional organizational structure is not well designed to enhance program diversity. It is difficult to fashion truly distinctive alternatives, for no single office or unit really controls the curriculum. A department influences that portion of a student's program taken in his major, but it is seldom able to fashion a total and cohesive undergraduate educational experience. Institutes could contribute to the development of more options, greater diversity, and broader choice among genuinely different alternatives than are presently available to students. External degree programs, ethnic study, and experientially based educational programs are only samples of the variety that might be introduced.

Persistent attempts have been made to develop and apply a program planning budgeting system (PPBS) in higher education. The reasons for such pressures are complex and reflect the increased costs of higher education, public consciousness of the growing tax dollars required by all levels of education, increased demands for public accountability, and a recognition by complex universities themselves of their inability to manage institutional programs and finances as effectively as they must.

135

Beyond Academic Departments

The need for PPB systems and the problems and slowness encountered in implementing them arise partly from a discipline-oriented structure. Most departments carry out many programs or parts of programs and thus universities have difficulty in increasing resources for one function—say undergraduate education—and reducing those for another. Departmental resources are allocated among functions largely by department chairmen and faculty members, well able to make certain kinds of professional judgments but ill-equipped to stand accountable to governing boards, coordinating councils, and legislative auditors. And allocation of funds among functions at the departmental level tends not to be a conscious decision; frequently, only cost studies can show where the money really went. It is increasingly difficult for public institutions to explain to legislators and others why monies appropriated for one purpose actually end up being used for something else. While one rarely intended deception or subterfuge, the end result is no less hard to defend. Increased use of the institute model, with narrower, more specific functional boundaries, deserves further study. Such application might make the connection between budgeting and programs more direct. Moreover, as university units accept greater responsibility for fewer functions, greater performance accountability might be obtained.

Institutes and centers multiplied rapidly on university campuses during the past decade and they provide an interesting and useful alternative to the academic department. Institutes are not likely to displace departments as the principal university organizational unit, but cautious increased use of the institute model could enable universities to attack certain problems which are difficult to handle through the conventional academic structure. The challenge is to minimize those shortcomings such as opportunism and goal displacement that characterize some institutes and centers and to apply generally and wisely those strengths of the institute structure that could lead to a more effective functioning of colleges and universities.

Bibliography

Academic Plan Steering Committee. "Academic Plan for the Berkeley Campus, 1968–1975." Berkeley: University of California, 1968.

American Council on Education. *Sponsored Research Policy of Colleges and Universities: A Report of the Committee on Institutional Research Policy.* Washington, D.C.: American Council on Education, 1954.

BAILEY, S. K. "Emergence of the Laboratory Program." *Journal of Research and Development in Education,* 1970, *3*(2), 5–17.

BARZUN, J. *The American University: How It Runs, Where It Is Going.* New York: Harper and Row, 1968.

BECKER, S., AND GORDON, G. "An Entrepreneurial Theory of Formal Organizations." *Administrative Science Quarterly,* 1966, *11,* 315–344.

BETZ, F., AND KRUYTBOSCH, C. "Sponsored Research and University Budgets: A Case Study in American University Government." *Minerva,* 1970, *8,* 492–519.

Carnegie Commission on Higher Education. *Less Time, More Options —Education Beyond the High School.* New York: McGraw-Hill, 1971.

CARTTER, A. M. *An Assessment of Quality in Graduate Education.* Washington, D.C.: American Council on Education, 1966.

CLARK, B. R. "Faculty Organization and Authority." In T. F. Lunsford (Ed.), *The Study of Academic Administration.* Boulder: Western Interstate Commission for Higher Education, 1963. Reprinted in H. M. Vollmer and D. L. Mills (Eds.), *Professionalization.* Englewood Cliffs, N.J.: Prentice-Hall, 1966, pp. 283–294.

DE WITT, L. B., AND TUSSING, A. D. *The Supply and Demand for Graduates of Higher Education: 1970 to 1980.* Syracuse, N.Y.: Syracuse University Research Corporation, 1971.

DRESSEL, P. L., AND FARICY, W. H. *Return to Responsibility.* San Francisco: Jossey-Bass, 1972.

DRESSEL, P. L., JOHNSON, F. C., AND MARCUS, P. M. "The Proliferating Institutes." *Change,* 1969, *1*(4), 21–24.

DRESSEL, P. L., JOHNSON, F. C., AND MARCUS, P. M. *The Confidence Crisis.* San Francisco: Jossey-Bass, 1970.

FRANCIS, W. L. *Legislative Issues in the Fifty States: Comparative Analysis.* Chicago: Rand McNally, 1967.

GROSS, E., AND GRAMBSCH, P. V. *University Goals and Academic Power.* Washington, D.C.: American Council on Education, 1968.

GROSS, N. "Organizational Lag in American Universities." *Harvard Educational Review,* 1963, *33*, 58–73.

HAWORTH, L. J. "Some Problems and Trends in the Support of Academic Science." In F. Seitz (Ed.), *Science, Government and the Universities.* Seattle: University of Washington Press, 1966.

IKENBERRY, S. O. *A Profile of Proliferating Institutes: A Study of Selected Characteristics of Institutes and Centers in 51 Land-Grant Universities.* University Park: The Pennsylvania State University Center for the Study of Higher Education, 1970.

JENCKS, C., AND RIESMAN, D. *The Academic Revolution.* Garden City, N.Y.: Doubleday, 1968.

KRUYTBOSCH, C., AND MESSINGER, S. L. "Unequal Peers: The Situation of Researchers at Berkeley," *The American Behavioral Scientist,* 1968, *11*, 33–43.

LITCHFIELD, E. H. "Organization in Large American Universities: The Faculties." *Journal of Higher Education,* 1959, *30*(7), 353–364.

MARCH, M. S. *Federal Budget Priorities for Research and Development.* Chicago: The University of Chicago Center for Policy Study, 1970.

MARTIN, W. B. *Conformity: Standards and Changes in Higher Education.* San Francisco: Jossey-Bass, 1969.

Bibliography

MASON, W. S., AND BOYAN, W. J. "Perspectives on Educational R&D Centers." *Journal of Research and Development in Education,* 1968, *1*(4), 190–202.

NESBET, R. *The Degradation of the Academic Dogma: The University in America, 1945–1970.* New York: Basic Books, 1971.

NEWMAN, F., AND ASSOCIATES. *Report on Higher Education.* Washington, D.C.: Government Printing Office, 1971.

NEWMAN, J. H. *The Idea of a University.* Edited by M. J. Svaglic. New York: Holt, Rinehart & Winston, 1960.

NORMAN, M. M. *Centers and Institutes at The Pennsylvania State University: A Case Study.* University Park: The Pennsylvania State University Center for the Study of Higher Education, 1971.

ORLANS, H. *The Nonprofit Research Institute.* New York: McGraw-Hill, 1972.

PALMER, A. M. (Ed.) *Research Centers Directory.* Detroit: Gale Research, 1968.

PORTER, H. W. "State University Policy on Establishment of Bureaus, Institutes, Centers, and Like Units at Institutions of the State University." Memorandum. Albany: The State University of New York, March 23, 1965.

RAND, C. *Cambridge USA: Hub of a New World.* New York: Oxford University Press, 1964.

RIVLIN, A. M. *The Role of the Federal Government in Financing Higher Education.* Washington, D.C.: The Brookings Institution, 1961.

ROSSI, P. H. "Researchers, Scholars and Policy Makers: The Politics of Large-Scale Research." *Daedalus,* 1964, *93,* 1142–1161.

SMITH, A. G. *Communication and Status: The Dynamics of a Research Center.* Eugene: The University of Oregon Center for the Advanced Study of Educational Administration, 1966.

STEINHART, J., AND CHERNIACK, S. *The Universities and Environmental Quality—Commitment to Problem-Focused Education.* Report to the President's Environmental Quality Council. Washington, D.C.: Government Printing Office, 1969.

University of California. "Policy of the University of California on Organized Research Units." Berkeley: University of California, 1963.

University of California. "Report of the Committee on Educational

Policy 1967–68." Berkeley: University of California, December 17, 1968.

University of Wisconsin. "Guideline: Academic Staff Positions, Appointments and Titles." 2nd ed. Madison: University of Wisconsin, 1970.

U. S. House of Representatives. 88th Cong., 2nd sess., 1964. *Congressional Record,* 110, pt. 9, 12453.

U. S. Office of Education. *Cooperative Research Programs: Application Instructions for Research Contracts, U. S. Department of Health, Education and Welfare.* Washington, D.C.: Government Printing Office, 1963.

U. S. Senate. Committee on Interior and Insular Affairs. *Water Resources Research Act. Hearings* on S.2, 88th Cong., 1st sess., February 19, 1963.

Utah State University. "Policy on Organized Research Units." Logan: Utah State University, 1968.

Index

A

Academic departments, 18; comparison of with institutes, 4, 102–106, 123–124; functions of, 101–102; power of, 60, 84–89, 122, 129

Academic reform, 23, 131, 133

Accountability, 42

Adaptive institutes, 36–37

Administration: of instruction, 58–59; of public service, 55; of research, 54

Advisory committees, 89–94, 122–123; composition of, 90–91; program control of, 93–94; role of, 91–92

Agricultural experiment stations, 78

Agricultural extension service, 55

American Association of Universities, 26

American Council on Education, 12, 137

Authority structure, 111

B

BACON, F., 98

BAILEY, S. K., 72

BARZUN, J., 112

BECKER, S., 33–34

B (cont.)

BETZ, F., 76

BOYAN, W. J., 71

C

Career satisfactions, 18, 117

Carnegie Commission on Higher Education, 135, 138

CARTTER, A. M., 25, 86

CHERNIACK, S., 84

CLARK, B. R., 22

Classified research, 114

Conflict resolution, 22

Controversy and criticism, 2–3, 110–112

Cooperative Research Act of 1964, 69

D

Data collection, 7–9

DEWITT, L. B., 10

Disciplinary homogeneity, 60

DRESSEL, P. L., 101, 125

E

Education centers and laboratories, 68–74; guidelines of, 70; origins of, 68–72; problems of, 73–74; regional, 72; as re-

141

Index

search and development centers, 70

Elementary and Secondary Education Act of 1965, 72

Entrepreneurship, 5, 11, 18, 41, 43, 112, 123, 126

F

Facilitation: of instruction, 57; of public service, 55; of research, 52–53

Faculty: appointment of, 31–33; loyalties of, 31–33; offices of, 31–33; role of in institutes, 50

FRANCIS, W. L., 66

Functions: of departments, 101–102; of institutes, 43, 109, 118–119, 129. *See also* Administration; Facilitation; Performance

G

Gardner Task Force on Education, 72

Goal displacement, 41

GORDON, G., 33–34

Graduate programs, 21, 57–58

GRAMBSCH, P. V., 99, 100

GROSS, E., 99, 100

H

Hatch Act, 87

HAWORTH, L. J., 13

I

IKENBERRY, S. O., 7, 79, 138

Informal collaboration, 15

Inquiry networks, 63, 68, 71, 80

Institutes and centers: career satisfaction in, 18, 117; comparison of with academic departments, 102–104, 123; controversy over, 2–3; evaluation of, 89, 126, 130; functions of, 109, 118–119, 129; history of, 1–2; integration of, 114–115;

mission of, 50; organizational structure of, 120–121; origins of, 11–28, 116; perquisites of, 5, 19; recruitment for, 20; support for, 27–28

Institutional development, 11–12, 19

Institutional visibility, 25

Integration, 114–115

Interdisciplinary collaboration, 14, 44–46; extent of, 47; models for, 45, 119; in physical and life science institutes, 47, 79; in social science-humanities institutes, 47–48; in water centers, 46–49

Issues, 114–115

J

JENCKS, C., 15, 17, 45

JOHNSON, F. C., 101, 125

JOHNSON, L. B., 72

K

KERR, C., 98

KEYNES, J. M., 77

KRUYTBOSCH, C., 76, 86

L

LITCHFIELD, E. H., 135

M

MAASS, A. W., 65

MARCH, M. S., 13

MARCUS, P. M., 101, 125

MARTIN, W. B., 135

MASON, W. S., 71, 139

MESSINGER, S. L., 86

Mission, 50

N

National Academy of Sciences, 64

National Association of State Universities and Land Grant Colleges, 68

National Defense Education Act, 68

National objectives, 11–28, 116

142

Index

Index

motives of, 20–23; perceptions of about institutes, 104–109; as respondents, 8–9

University purposes, 11, 98–99, 115, 124

U.S. Office of Education, 70, 73, 74

W

Water centers: advisory committee of, 93; assessment of, 67–68; financing of, 66, 80–81; functions of, 51, 54; inclusion of, 7; interdisciplinary involvement of, 46–49; legislation and, 67; origins of, 13, 65; structure of, 36–37

Water Resources Act of 1964, 64–66

WOLMAN, A., 64

World War II, 2, 4, 17, 79, 98, 113